Progressive Logic:
Framing A Unified Field Theory of Values For Progressives

William J. Kelleher, Ph. D.

EMPATHIC SCIENCE INSTITUTE
LOS ANGELES, CALIFORNIA

To Henry, Bob and Helen

TABLE OF CONTENTS

INTRODUCTION

Lakoff Lacks Logic

For those who are unfamiliar with George Lakoff's book *Don't Think of an Elephant*, we will mention its main points in a moment. But first, as the title of this Introduction suggests, we see in that little book a great deficiency. While Lakoff sincerely desires to further the cause of progressivism, he utterly fails to state the basic premise that gives meaning to the progressive project. He takes a "their side vs. our side" stance, but without persuasively showing why his side is preferable.

We will argue here that the progressive view is preferable to the conservative alternative, precisely because of progressivism's basic value premise and the logical and political implications of that premise. We will state that basic premise. We will also set out the four logical axioms that can be derived from it. Our central thesis is that this set of principles has moved progressives in the past, moves them now, and will continue to do so in the future. We will argue that progressives ought to frame future policy debates in the terms of this "progressive logic." If that is done, we predict that a substantial portion of formerly conservative voters will shift their allegiance to the progressive side. We are so confident in the persuasive power of progressive logic as to further claim that it could empower progressives to enact a reform agenda for the 21st Century that will dwarf the New Deal in importance.

Before making our case, however, let us ask a few

questions to set the philosophical context in which we write. Our central concern is with the process of valuing. For example, how does one know the value of oneself, of others, or of anything else? Is money the only standard of value, at least for Americans? Are people equivalent in value to the things of this Earth, whether animal, mineral, or vegetable? Or, are we of lesser, or greater, value than things? Indeed, there are people who value their car, or their pet dog, way above their neighbor. There are corporate CEOs and shareholders who value their profits above the lives of those who are injured or killed driving unsafe cars, taking inadequately tested medication, or smoking cigarettes.

Are there any value contradictions in these cases, or are all valuations equal and every one free to value as he or she pleases in the moment?

Our view is that human beings have, in varying degrees, an innate value intuition. We will further explain that notion in this essay. Readers with a stronger intuition will have already seen clearly the value contradictions in those instances we have mentioned. These readers will agree that people should be regarded as more important than things. Readers with a weaker intuition may argue that all values are relative to a particular culture, group, or to the whims of the individual. In this relativistic view, the values that persist in a society are those which power and tradition enforce. But if values have no basis other than political power and custom, then what is our defense against the claim that might makes right?

Many people intuitively reject the notion that might makes right. Something seems askew in the claim of kings and tyrants that people are to be valued merely as pawns in the game of politics. In this essay, democracy is our ideal. But is the democratic valuation of individual dignity only "right" because it is in the self-interest of the masses, who fear the domination of the few? Or, do democratic values have deeper roots in a more solid foundation?

We will argue that American progressives have been moved to advocate and advance democratic reforms in the U.S. by their value intuition far more so than by any calculation of self-interest. As we will show, progressive activists have succeeded in politics mostly by stirring up the same value intuitions in the American public.

George Lakoff is a writer with a strong progressive value intuition. In *Don't Think of an Elephant*, he recognizes that progressives are currently in the political doldrums. He argues that progressive values can be more successfully advanced if greater care is taken in the way progressives frame their agenda. Words are the engine of politics. Words are the most effective instrument progressives have for evoking public support and enthusiasm for their candidates and policies. Conservatives owe their current political success largely to the way they have framed their policies so as to appeal to the majority of voters. They have shrewdly put their policies and candidates in positive frames, and progressive policies and candidates in negative frames.

We find this part of Lakoff's argument indisputable. However, when he presents the intellectual foundation for his progressive values, we think, he falls on his face. His theory that personality types are the source of

American values is, for us, both intellectually unsatisfying and politically unhelpful. He argues, in effect, that there are two basic personality types afloat in the United States. One is attracted to the values of the "nurturing parent." The other is attracted to the values of a "strict father." Since everyone has a little bit of both types in them, progressives have an even chance of moving the voters to vote progressive by being more clever than the conservatives at framing.

He seems to be suggesting that progressive candidates should artfully assume the posture of a "nurturing parent." By framing their campaigns in this fashion, he implies, the progressive candidates will trigger the unconscious need in a majority of voters to have a "nurturing parent" in public office. Aside from the lack of empirical evidence for his thesis, imagine Hillary Clinton, John Kerry, John Edwards, Jesse Jackson, or even Dennis Kucinich proclaiming to the crowds "I want to be your nurturing parent!"

That just won't fly. In fact, many grown-ups will feel offended. The candidate would look condescending. Their efforts to by-pass the adult reasoning processes of the voters, so as to manipulate some supposed unconscious need, would make them appear as sneaky, unprincipled, and out of touch with human reality.

We agree with Lakoff's assumption that progressives are sorely in need of an intellectual foundation for their shared sense of humane values. But we see his venture into pop psychology as a non-starter.

While Lakoff's efforts to find a basis for progressive values rely on a pseudo-science, there are some widely read religious alternatives. Some liberal Christian preachers are taking a wealth of quotes from the Bible in an attempt to provide an intellectual foundation for the progressive value intuition. Other men of the cloth attempt to assure progressives that based on their personal conversations with The Lord, He is definitely a "liberal." However, we find the religious effort to justify the humane value intuition of progressives not only intellectually unsatisfying, but *dangerous*. We will elaborate on this view in the latter half of our essay.

Despite these criticisms, the reader will see that our essay is not about putting down religion or pop psychology. It is about putting forth an explanation as to why progressive values are intellectually far superior to the values of their political rivals on the right. Our aim here is to provide a "frame" for progressive values that will command widespread respect. Indeed, we think we have such a convincing intellectual framework that activists will be moved to go out and tell the people about it, and around which candidates will center their speeches. The truth of these claims is for you to decide.

You be the judge.

Chapter One:
What is Progressive Logic?

Confusion Abounds

In our view, the American progressive movement has suffered from a severe lack of unity and consistency. This has been due above all to the failure of its leaders, elected officials, intellectuals, and activists to clearly articulate the basic principles that have moved them. Ironically, they have acted without understanding fully the deepest reasons for their own activity. In the absence of this depth self-understanding they have failed to see the ultimate principles that they have shared. While the issues and activists have changed over time, these principles have remained the underlying motivating force; albeit unbeknownst to the actors. Hence, unless an immediate project has held them together, like abolition, the Civil War, the need to ameliorate the unconscionable exploitation of workers, including women and children, or to engage in anti-war protests, or to fight for civil rights, progressive activists have been unable to agree upon their unifying values.

Lacking an articulated logic of values, progressives have had to operate with only an intuitive sense of values. Small wonder, then that they have been so disorganized and sporadic in their political successes. How could they have based a lasting organization upon an intuition, which is only now being articulated and clarified? Organizing around an intuitive understanding of values has proven all but impossible. Like the four blind men standing around that elephant we are not

supposed to think of, each one has a different
understanding. "An elephant is like a rope," says the
man holding its tail. "No, an elephant is like a great
snake," asserts the man who is stroking the trunk. "Not
at all," counters the man running his hands up and down
a leg, "an elephant is like a tree." "How could you be so
foolish," declares the man who slides his hands over the
side of the creature, "an elephant is most surely like a
great wall."

So progressivism has been scattered into factions such
as Abolitionists, Populists, Socialists, Republican "Bull
Moose," Democratic "liberals," Greens, and other
groups that could not see the unified field of values in
which they all operated. Like the Supreme Court
Justices who declare that they will know "obscenity"
when they see it, progressives have been trying to
pressure government to shape America into a form that
they will know is "just" when they see it. Unfortunately,
the value intuition upon which they have been relying
fragments into separate notions as they try to translate it
into policy. Once competitive egos organize around
rival ideas and personalities, all contact with the
unifying field is lost. In Zen this is called "The
Philosopher's Disease."

As the 21st Century begins unfolding into the future,
progressives seem more fragmented and mired in
bickering than at any time in their past. At the same
time, our conservative opponents have rarely been so
well organized. They have a huge share of the
judgeships on the federal bench, a majority on the
Supreme Court, and majorities in both houses of
Congress. Their share of state and local offices has
never been so large. Finally, from the progressive

perspective, one of the worst presidents in American history is now serving his second term.

Fortunately, this sorry situation can be turned around. With a unified field theory of values, progressive activists will be able to see for themselves, and articulate to others, what has been impelling their movement from its inception. Hence, the possibility for a stronger and better organized left now exists as it has never before existed. With an understanding of progressive logic, our side will no longer be limited to the chance confluence of events to give momentary vitality and direction to the movement. Progressive logic will give progressives the tools they need to become a permanent power in American politics.

Progressive logic, then, has no history as such, but only a pre-history. That pre-history is one of an intuitive understanding seeking expression through political reform, but without full success, for over 200 years. This essay is the realization of what progressive logic has been, for so long, wanting; that is, its own articulation. For, now that it has been stated (in effect, born), the history of progressive logic can begin.

Our Basic Premise:
All persons always deserve positive regard

The basic premise of progressive logic is deceptively simple. Yet, as we will see, in practice it contains enormous power for clarifying thought, framing policy debates, and persuading people to agree with its conclusions. Four value axioms can be deduced from the premise that all persons always deserve positive regard. After stating these axioms, we will further discuss their meanings. We will also anticipate some of the objections that readers may raise as they read the premise; especially the objection "I don't feel that 'all persons always deserve positive regard.' Sometimes I feel that some people deserve my negative regard." Let this essay be a test of just how persuasive progressive logic can be.

Here are the four value axioms, two negative and two positive: 1st the Ideological Fallacy. 2d the Instrumental Fallacy. 3d the opposite of the ideological fallacy is Ideological Enhancement. 4th the opposite of the instrumental fallacy is Instrumental Enhancement.

What is the Ideological Fallacy? In short, it is the false assumption that ideas are more important than are persons. "Race," for example, is an intellectual construct, or a conception, as opposed to something that has an actual physical existence in reality. It is used to separate members of the human community, and to enable some to claim superiority over others. Indeed, the very idea of "human" becomes a system of ranking by which some "races" are deemed less human than others.

In racism, preserving the idea of race becomes more important than the actual person who is classified, or captured, by the category. For example, in the pre-Civil War South the idea of race had to be preserved to justify the white man's ownership of his black slaves. The concept was preserved at the cost to its victims of suffering and humiliation.

Gender bias entails the same kind of contradiction. Men in the United States once adhered to the intellectual construct that women were too weak and delicate to work in a "man's world." As a result, women were denied equal opportunities in education and careers. Of course, at that very time women worked as hard as men on farms, or drudging across the Western plains and deserts along with men in wagon trains, or read, wrote, and used mathematics as well as men in schools.

All this evidence to the contrary had to be ignored to preserve the conceptions of male gender superiority. The ideological fallacy generally includes some element of the psychological denial of reality to sustain itself. Indeed, slavery was sometimes justified as being *good* for the slaves, because it supposedly gave them a better life than they were intellectually able to give themselves. This self-deception, of course, rested upon a psychological denial of two very important facts. One is that the experience of slave life was painfully humiliating and degrading, not "good." The other is that blacks have as much innate ability to manage their own lives as do whites. In this fallacy, The Idea is given value supremacy even over reality!

Hence, the ideological fallacy entails subordinating the regard given a real person in favor of some idea, conception, system, or other kind of cognitive construct. If all persons always deserve positive regard, then logically no mere concept can be used as an excuse to diminish another person's value. We will discuss the operation of the ideological fallacy further, after we have given some nutshell definitions of the other three axioms.

What is the Instrumental Fallacy? To use a person solely as a means to achieving some end entails a negative regard for that person. Using reduces a person to the value of a thing, or an instrument. But under progressivism's basic premise, a person's value is different in kind than the value of a thing. No matter how highly prized in the moment, a thing is always potential trash. Every new car, for example, will one day lose its glamour and usefulness. Then its value will be diminished to that of junk.

But a person, so long as he or she is a self-conscious, thinking, feeling human being ought, under our basic premise, never be valued as useless trash. It is precisely the "all" and the "always" in our premise that raises the value of persons to being different in kind from that of things. The positive regard of things is always contingent upon their condition and their utility. But the positive regard of persons is unconditional; that is, given freely because they are persons. Hence, any valuation of a person as a thing commits the instrumental fallacy. This is an error of value logic because it is inconsistent with our basic premise. In a moment, we will discuss some examples of the instrumental fallacy in practice, such as child labor. (Violence is the worst form of the instrumental fallacy, because it reduces the person to the status of an object as well as inflicting physical injury.)

What is an Ideological Enhancement? The idea, eloquently stated by Martin Luther King, Jr., that a person should be judged by the content of his character rather than the color of his skin, is an example of ideological enhancement. It is an idea, or intellectual construct, that tends to encourage giving positive regard to people; therefore, it enhances the basic premise that all persons always deserve positive regard. In King's view, even the racists against whom he protested deserve respect as humans. That is why he never sanctioned the use of violence against them.

The public policy principle that all people, no matter what race, gender, religion, or national origin deserve an equal opportunity for education and career, is another instance of an ideological enhancement. This notion has long been a core element of the progressive movement. Here is a public policy that expresses the positive regard required by progressive logic. To assert that all persons always deserve an equal opportunity for education and career is clearly a consistent extension of our basic premise that all persons always deserve positive regard. We will discuss further examples of ideological enhancement throughout this essay.

What is an Instrumental Enhancement? Providing a service to people that helps to improve the quality of their lives is an example of an instrumental enhancement. Public education, for instance, processes students through an institutional system. Putting students through the educational process is a form of using them, but, however imperfectly, it is done in a way that is meant to enhance the quality of their lives. A student is not like a car on an assembly line precisely because the student, ideally, is valued as a unique, intelligent, creative, and sentient person, while the car is a thing valued only for its utility.

In principle, though again not necessarily in practice, putting a person who has been convicted of a crime into prison for "rehabilitation" is an instance of an instrumental enhancement. That the process often only "warehouses" people rather than rehabilitating them indicates a problem in the workings of the system more than a failure of the ideal. (We will return to this particular subject later.)

A surgeon cutting open a person's chest to repair a faulty heart is treating the person like a thing, just as a roasted turkey is treated on Thanksgiving Day. But the doc is doing his job in a way that is intended to enhance the patient's quality of life. By its value structure, then, a surgical operation is also an instance of instrumental enhancement.

These two major fallacies and two major enhancements derive directly from our basic premise that all persons always deserve positive regard. Together these five items constitute the core of the progressive project. That project is to give effect to the basic premise by deconstructing contradictions and by instituting enhancements.

The history of progressivism in America is the story of how, and how well, progressives have carried out their common project. We will see that the results have been uneven, and work on the project often disrupted, primarily because progressives have been unaware of these core elements underlying and informing their aims. Progressive programs and proposals have always assumed an implicit logic. But because this logic has not been brought to the forefront of progressive thought, it has not been applied or followed consistently. As a result, internecine warfare has obstructed unified action, and progressives are left with the frustrating feeling that we have something in common, but know not what. The common value intuition of progressives has not been a steady guide to sustained political action in the past. However, a clear statement of progressive principles can provide activists with an unshakeable unity of purpose that will sustain them far into the future.

The following presentation of progressive logic, in the context of historical action, will clarify the premises that have shaped progressive thinking from the old anti-slavery days through the labor movement, the New Deal, the fight for civil rights, and the protest against poverty, oppression, and unjust war. Some reforms will be suggested here. But our focus will be primarily on illustrating that many of the existing proposals and programs for progressive reforms can be seen as a part of a unified field. Armed with an understanding of the unifying logic of progressive thought, the seemingly arbitrary association of *this* program and *that* policy proposal can be eliminated. Once our logic is made clear, we progressives will be able to speak with one voice. That, in turn, will make us much easier to hear and far more convincing than the current cacophony of voices.

What Are Values?

Values are not the same as concepts or ideas, but are expressions of relative import. Thus, given all the existing ideas about what is good for a society, progressives value some of those ideas and conservatives value others. For example, one fundamental principle for progressives is that government should protect the unfettered right of workers to organize their own collective bargaining units, or unions. Conservatives, on the other hand, value the idea of "free enterprise." That idea entails the principle that business should be unfettered by unions.

Neither of these principles is, in our sense of the word, a

"value." They are ideas to which different people attribute different degrees of importance. Unionization is "valued," or considered preferable, by progressives. It is "disvalued," or regarded as repugnant, by conservatives. Our concern in this essay is to explain the logic followed by these different acts of valuing, and thus to account for the differences.

Valuing is not the mere expression of some transient emotion, or the arbitrary clinging to the nearest position on the spectrum of opinions. It is a form of thinking, or reasoning. It entails intellectual judgments about how various ideas, things, and actions relate to basic premises. Progressives and conservatives value differently because they start from different premises. The key terms to explain these differences in valuing are the "all" and "always" in the premise that all persons always deserve positive regard.

Conservatives, too, have a value premise, which is rarely, if ever, articulated. It is that "some people deserve our positive regard sometimes, and some people deserve our negative regard sometimes, and we are free to say who and when." Not only is this premise unpredictable in its attribution of value, but its operation requires a regal self-centeredness that is absent in the operation of the progressive premise. The conservative premise reserves to itself the kind of power that kings in fables and fairytales have. That is, the power of an Old Testament God, or the power of a Zeus high upon Mount Olympus. Conservatives covet the power to condemn other people at will. Their premise is practiced by the Queen of Hearts in *Alice in Wonderland*.

The progressive premise inhibits, rather than indulges, the personal power to cast condemning judgments on other people. The terms "all" and "always" require self-restraint and self-discipline. It is not always easy to hold oneself to the standard that all persons always deserve positive regard. To follow the progressive premise requires a far more humble mind than the haughty mind cultivated by the conservative premise. Clearly, the progressive premise is far more consistent with the ideal of democracy than is its autocratic conservative counterpart.

People of a more moderate predisposition may try to claim greater wisdom than the two extremes of progressivism and conservatism. But this is a self-deception. Moderates do have an implicit value premise. It is that "most people may deserve positive regard most of the time, but we will be the judge of who and when." But moderate autocracy is still autocracy. In part, as a result of this premise, moderates more often support conservative candidates and policies in their voting behavior than they do those of progressives. Fortunately, because they are more predisposed to attribute positive regard, moderates are more amenable to persuasion than are gung-ho conservatives, and therefore should be the main targets of progressive efforts to win more voters to our side.

We will discuss the political challenges facing progressives, and how to overcome them, later in this essay. First, let us review some of the major conflicts between conservatives and progressives in American history. In doing this, our main aim will be simply to illustrate how the competing value premises of the two sides have played out in the practice of politics.

Chapter Two:
Instances from History

Abolition

In the 30 years preceding the Civil War, abolitionist efforts intensified. The Underground Railroad was ushering hundreds of people into free territory. Many writers, like William Lloyd Garrison, and advocates on the speech circuit, such as Frederick Douglas and Wendell Phillips, worked full time to keep the issue on the front burner. Women's groups were expanding their demands to include black liberation as well as their own liberation.

Throughout this period no one articulated the elements of progressive logic. Yet, in our view, an intuitive sense of that logic moved these activists towards a common end. In the absence of a clear statement of progressive logic, progressives in the past sought language in their minds that would metaphorically express what intuition made them feel; that is, that slavery was an abomination, a travesty on human dignity and human rights. Now that we have an articulated statement of what progressive logic is, we can see in hindsight that our activist brothers and sisters assumed and acted upon that logic. When we reinterpret the past from the new point of view of progressive logic, we can see factors operating then that have only become visible now.

Consider "slavery" as a concept. Slavery entails the notion that a person can be owned, bought, and sold as personal property. Here is an instance of both the ideological fallacy and, in practice, the instrumental fallacy. Preserving the idea of a person as property was regarded by conservative pro-slavers as more important than the consequences the notion had on actual persons. And this idea did have consequences on real people. The writings of slaves and former slaves about their experience as chattels, or moveable property, uniformly show that they suffered painful humiliation. Indeed, they daily suffered a degree of physical and emotional trauma that no person in a civilized society should ever be made to endure.

Typically, this ideological fallacy blinded white southerners to the reality right in front of them. White southerners observed slaves dancing and singing, and self-servingly concluded that the slaves are a happy lot. In response to that myth, one former slave wrote that when they danced and sang it was not out of merriment, but "'to keep our hearts from being completely broken.'" [1] A slave named J. W. Logue escaped to free territory a few years before the Civil War. The woman who owned him wrote to him demanding $1000 compensation, and reminded him that she raised him along with her own children. He replied in an abolitionist newspaper, The Liberator, "'Woman, did you raise your own children for the market? ... Shame on you!'" [2]

Clearly, Mr. Logue is protesting against being valued by her as a piece of property. His protest expresses an intuitive understanding of the instrumental fallacy; that is, that when a person is valued as a thing, progressive logic's basic premise is contradicted. Human dignity

---

[1] Quoted in Howard Zinn, *A People's History of the United States*, 1995, page 168
[2] Ibid, page 177.

naturally demands that one always be treated with positive regard. Anything less is a painfully disturbing insult.

As we see it, much, if not most, of the popular protest against slavery came from an intuitive grasp of progressive logic's basic value premise. To be sure, there was some less value-sensitive economic incentive to call for the end of slavery. Northern "captains of industry" saw the unsettled Western territories as an opportunity to enlarge their markets and their profits by expanding their way of life into the West. Southern plantation owners saw in the West fertile land needed to replace the soil in the South then being exhausted by cotton. The Southerners wanted the West open to slave labor, not wage labor. The Northerners wanted wage laborers in the West so that the people would have money to buy their products. Hence, Northern elites had a pecuniary reason to oppose slavery in the South. But the greed of elites alone cannot explain the strong motivation of the Northern people to fight a civil war to end slavery.

That progressive logic was unknown to abolitionists exacerbated the problems of the time. Because value sensitive people then were unable to frame the issue as one of value logic, the debate frame defaulted to other forms. William Lloyd Garrison is an example of how one default frame became prominent among progressives. In the first issue of The Liberator, his weekly abolitionist newspaper, he proclaimed "I will be harsh as truth and as uncompromising as justice. ... I will not equivocate. ... I will not retreat a single inch – AND I WILL BE HEARD." Thus, he became the leading spokesman for the moralistic frame. That is, he framed the debate in terms of absolute morality; slavery was bad and emancipation good PERIOD!

Following the logic of moral superiority, Garrison publicly burnt a copy of the Constitution for being too supportive of slavery. On at least one occasion, he was dragged off the stage and beaten by people he angered. But he did inspire others to become activists. They spoke and wrote against slavery with equal moral fervor. They visited churches and homes, and organized meetings. Thoreau published his essay on civil disobedience during this period, and Emerson also encouraged abolitionist activism. Activist efforts produced nearly 2000 abolitionist groups by 1840.

Activism works, but not always for the best. The fiery rhetoric of moral absolutists like Garrison, plus increasing acts of violence like Nat Turner's slave revolt and John Brown's raid at Harpers Ferry, had the undesirable consequence of helping to solidify Southern opposition. We will argue further in a moment that progressives could have exploited the moderates in the South rather than drive those moderates to the conservative extreme by forcing them into the category of the "bad people," (or as George Bush II would later say of terrorists, "the evil ones").

When the debate is framed in terms of moral absolutes, the possibilities for mutual understanding are greatly diminished. The frame itself requires each participant to strive for ever higher moral ground than the opponent's. Each side tries to demonize the other, rather than to seek common ground upon which to base a peaceful resolution of their differences.

A special form of the moralistic frame used then was the "liberty frame." For example, in the absence of progressive logic, many abolitionists rationalized their passion to liberate slaves on the grounds that all people have the right to "liberty." Climbing to higher moral ground, Southerners simply turned "liberty" against the Northerners. "Liberty" entitles the Southerners to live their chosen way of life without Northern meddling. Because "liberty" is such a nebulous conception, it could be used in opposite ways without providing any intellectual basis for resolution by reason. Lincoln felt the frustration caused by the plasticity of that word. In 1845 he wrote "I hold it a paramount duty of us in the free states, and perhaps to liberty itself (paradox though it may seem), to let the slavery of other states alone." [3]

Excuse me?! In the name of "liberty," Lincoln would let slavery continue in the Southern states! Clearly, the idea of "liberty" had nothing to contribute to a clarification of the issues.

The religious frame was no more useful. Northern Christians argued that the slaves should be freed because "we are all God's creations, and should therefore treat one another equally and respectfully." Southern Christians dodged that argument by claiming that "God has charged the morally superior European white man with the heavy burden of civilizing his inferior African brothers." Southern Christian preachers quoted the Bible, where Saint Paul says "Servants, obey

---

[3] Quoted in Richard Hofstadter, *The American Political Tradition,* 1948, 1974. At that time, Lincoln was content to contain slavery to the South, keep it out of the West, and hope it would die "a natural death."

your master." Northerners were fond of the "Good Samaritan" story.

America was headed straight towards the worst catastrophe it has ever had to endure, and the religious frame was pathetically useless at clarifying the issues or leading the minds of the day to a peaceful resolution of their differences. As Lincoln noted, God was on both sides, and the United States became a house divided against itself.

To fully understand the function of frames, one must recognize a distinction between thought and feeling. Feeling can precede thought in a person's consciousness. Words, language, or thought can express these preceding feelings, as metaphors for the feelings. We introduce an articulated progressive logic here as an alternative frame to those frames that were actually used by progressive abolitionists. The moralistic frame, the liberty frame, and the religious frame combined prior to the Civil War to fire the sentiment in both North and South that made the war possible. Hence, let no one doubt the importance of frames for influencing events.

Of course, activists using frames do not operate in a vacuum. Those who blame abolitionist activism for stirring up war fever, such as historian Avery Craven, fail to explain why so many people responded to the abolitionist rhetoric, rather than simply passing it by. The words themselves would be mere marks on paper, and sounds in the air, but for the value sensitivity of the people. So, it was the value intuition of the people that gave saliency to the abolitionist propaganda. That propaganda was a metaphor expressing the intuitive awareness in the people of a natural order of values within them. In our opinion, this natural order of values finds its purest and most precise expression in progressive logic. The moralistic frame also expresses that value intuition, but with undesirable consequences in practice, such as being able to supply both sides with an uncompromising position.

Unfortunately, no one spoke more clearly for progressives than did Garrison when he wrote, "our object is *universal emancipation*, to redeem women as well as men from a servile to an equal condition." The attraction of this quote, and those like it, for progressives is that it expresses their intensely felt value intuition that all persons always deserve positive regard. But the drawback of such high sounding language is that it leaves no room for patient discussion, negotiation, or compromise. Either "universal emancipation" exists, or we are all enslaved. Either Southerners give up their way of life without delay and without compensation, or fight a war.

While moralists like Garrison, Phillips, and others had strong value sensitivity, they made a framing error when translating their intuition into words. They translated their sense of values into moral absolutes, and that frame then took on a logic of its own. Those whom they inspired committed the same mistake. It was a mistake because the frame itself led to consequences that were inconsistent with the original value intuition that all persons always deserve positive regard. In other words, well-intentioned people chose a misleading frame through which to assert their good intentions. The combination of their moralistic frame, the liberty frame, and the religious frame eventually prevailed, but at an awful cost in human life and suffering. They won;

hence, they can claim to have been "right." But was the game worth the candle?

This may come as some surprise, but the abolitionists, like Garrison, committed the same error of progressive logic as did the slave owners whom they fought. We have said that to preserve the idea of slavery despite the pain it caused other people is an instance of the ideological fallacy – ideas are never more important than real persons. Yet, to hold up the airy notion of "universal emancipation" as a justification for killing Southerners is just as much an instance of the ideological fallacy. There were alternatives to this high-sounding excuse for murder.

The frame of a debate can influence the mood of the discourse. By framing the debate in terms of logic, the opponents are more likely to be in a reasonable mood than they would be if the frame is "my brilliant interpretation of 'liberty' versus your stupid one," or who's side God is on today. When advocates engage one another as reasonable people the way to reach a reasonable settlement is more likely to be open than it would be if both sides insist upon positions for which there is no middle ground.

A debate in the frame of logic requires that both sides see and treat one another as rational beings. Hence, opponents begin from a position of respect for each other's mental faculties. This position can help to keep the dispute from degenerating into one of "offended ego against offended ego." Also, by relying on logic, the worst consequences of other frames are avoided. The meaninglessness of the term "liberty," divisive moralizing, and the comical hypocrisy of Christianity guarantee that opposing views will quickly slip into strong emotion and rigid stances without any intellectual guidance towards a reasonable conclusion.

Suppose the abolitionists had had a fully articulated progressive logic. They could have declared their basic premise that all persons always deserve positive regard. They could have analyzed slavery as both an ideological and an instrumental fallacy, as we did above. Pro-slavers would then have had two ways to defend slavery. One would have been to deny that Africans were "persons." Many whites of both North and South did just that. The other defense would have had to assert the right to pick and choose to whom they would attribute positive and negative regard.

These two issues stem from framing the debate in the terms of progressive logic. Each side, respecting the rationality of the other, would have to make arguments that appeal to reason. Compare these two issues with the issues raised by the other three frames we discussed above. They offered no intellectual guidance, and no opportunity for increased mutual understanding. The intellectual emptiness of those frames left a vacuum that only emotion and willfulness could fill. The intensity of Southern resistance came from the way they defined their situation. They understood themselves as being challenged to defend "the Southern way of life" or "surrender unconditionally to the tyranny of the North." This "liberty" frame dictated the only conclusion open to the South – "live free or die!"

But a rational, logic-based debate over whether or not blacks are real people would have been far less worth dying for to whites than was the defense of their way of life. And a full blown debate about the differences between the progressive basic premise and the conservative basic premise would have little chance of motivating millions to take up arms and even oppose members of their own families.

Thus, framing the debate in the terms of progressive logic can defuse the kind of intensity that leads to murderous rage. With feelings tempered and minds in a more reasonable mood, programs for change can be advanced against less rigid resistance.

Long before emotions got out of control, Southern leadership had already acquiesced in passing laws that were sure to reduce, if not phase out, slavery over time. Section 9 of Article One in the U. S. Constitution empowered Congress to prohibit the importation of slaves after 1808. This was, in effect, about a 20-year advance notice to the South that slavery in the United States faced a gradual phasing out. Without importation, domestic slave breeding would not be able to meet the planter's demand for more slaves. They would eventually have to move to a wage system, especially to slow the amount of slaves running away to free territories. Yet, by 1789 the colonies of both North and South had ratified the Constitution with that provision in it. And, in 1808 Congress did outlaw the importation of slaves. That the South accepted this federal regulation of slavery at the time of forming the Union, and let that law be passed in Congress in 1808, suggests that substantial moderate sentiment existed in the South.

As late as 1832 the Virginia legislature considered a bill that would have gradually emancipated the slaves in that state. It was defeated by a 73 to 58 vote. On the positive side, this measure received the support of 45% of the legislators who voted on the issue. Those lawmakers represented thousands of moderate Virginians. Virginia then was a very influential state in the South. It had produced four of America's first five presidents. It had the potential to be a strong voice for moderation and reason.

If progressives had famed the debate in the terms of progressive logic, they might have been able to increase the influence of moderates among the pro-slavers. Shoving every Southerner's back against the wall with uncompromising moralizing cut off that possibility. If moderation had been encouraged by engaging Southerners as rational beings capable of reasonable discourse, rather than as moral monsters who had to be shot in the defense of humanity, a reasonable atmosphere may have made other options than war more achievable.

One example of an ideological enhancement that was being floated at the time was for the federal government to buy out the slaves. Section 8 of Article One gives Congress the power to tax to pay for "the common defense and general welfare of the United States." If progressives had pushed this program in Congress while engaging the South in rational discourse, resistance to emancipation could have been decreased as moderates began accepting monetary compensation for relinquishing their "ownership" rights over slaves. This money would have helped former slave owners make the transition from relying on slave labor to employing wage laborers.

Former slaves, too, could have been paid "back wages" by the United States. This would have enabled emancipated persons to choose freely whether to stay and work the fields for pay, or relocate. Western territories were open to settlement, and northern states could easily have absorbed black migration into both their rural and urban areas.

There would likely have been several holdouts, who would not sell "their" slaves at any price. Their egos were too invested in their special privileges. But they would not have found any allies in the moderates who had taken federal funds and were adjusting to their new conditions. Stubborn stick-in-the-muds could have been compelled to see reason by the courts, rather than by an invading army. The Constitution allows government to take property if done with "due process of law."

Of course, such a buy-out approach seems to be "morally impure" because it creates the appearance of technically validating the notion of slaves as property. However, in practice it would have been an instrumental enhancement because it has the virtue of both respecting Southern whites, however misguided their beliefs, and freeing the slaves without needless violence. That consequence would have been consistent with the basic premise of progressive logic that all persons always deserve positive regard. Tragically, minds that were possessed by the passions of moral superiority, on both sides, opposed this program.

As further evidence of the influence moderates had in the pre-war period, consider the Missouri Compromise. In 1820, the members of Congress agreed to allow Maine to enter the Union as a free state, and to allow

Missouri in as a slave state. They also agreed that some
territories would stay free and that others could be
allowed into the Union as slave. While war rhetoric was
heating up on both sides, moderation prevailed.

Twenty years later, a slave named Dred Scott sued his
owner in federal court saying that because he had been
taken into a free territory by his owner, he had become
free under Congress's law. The Supreme Court took the
case in 1856, and handed down its decision in 1857. To
the astonishment and horror of progressives, the Court
declared that slaves are not citizens, but property. As
such, they have no right to sue. So, Dred Scott had no
standing to sue for his freedom. Scott never attained
freedom, declared the High Court, because Congress
had no authority to make the Missouri Compromise in
the first place. That law deprived slave owners of their
property without due process, and in violation of the
Constitution. Wherever Scott was taken, he remained
property, and Congress could do nothing about it! (So
forget about that buy out program.)

Here is the conservative premise guiding judicial
activism. Six of the seven Justices on the majority were
Southern pro-slavers. Also, the opinion affirmed as a
matter of law that slaves were not "persons," but only
property under the U. S. Constitution. That put an end to
any progressives effectively arguing that blacks are
"persons." Now the good Christian Southerners did not
even have to argue that it was their Christian duty to
raise the level of humanity in blacks – the Supreme
Court had just removed black people from the category
"human"! This is the ultimate form of the ideological
fallacy – the imperious declaration that simply by the

Court's fiat some human beings are no longer "human beings."

Here was enshrined into Constitutional law the conservative principle that they reserve the right to declare who is and isn't deserving of positive regard. Their reading of the Constitution made negative regard for black people required as the law of the land. "Off with their humanity!" The Queen of Hearts was no longer in Wonderland; she was in Washington, D.C.

Thus, the *Dred Scott* decision put an end to any hope that after 1857 progressive logic could have played a role in diverting the nation's march to war. But this will not be the last time that conservative High Court Justices demonstrate value blindness and insensitivity to progressive logic.

The Civil War began three years later. It lasted until 1865. In that year the 13th Amendment was ratified, and slavery was outlawed in the U.S. Then in 1868, the 14th Amendment was ratified, effectively overturning the *Dred Scott* opinion, and giving the rights of "due process" and "equal protection" to all persons. These amendments are examples of how governments can express positive regard for the people.

Child Labor and Public Education:
The Changing Meanings of "Positive Regard"

Attitudes towards child labor in the U.S. have changed over the past few hundred years. William Bradford, governor of Plymouth Colony from 1621 to 1657,

observed then that child labor was both an element of
the Puritan ethic of industry and a "necessitie."
Necessary because they had seen "the grime and grisly
face of povertie coming upon them."

Progressive Edith Abbott studied attitudes towards child
labor in early American history. The Bradford quote
came from an article by Abbott published in a 1908
edition of the American Journal of Sociology.[4] She
quotes Bradford further as a witness to the effects of
child labor. Putting their children to work, as young as
age 8, in the fields and mills of New England writes
Bradford,

> did not a little wound ye tender hearts of many a
> loving father and mother, so it produced likewise
> sundrie sad and sorrowful effects. For many of their
> children ... haveing lernde to bear ye yoake in their
> youth, and willing to bear parte of their parents'
> burden, were, oftentimes, so oppressed with their
> hevie labours that though their minds were free and
> willing, yet their bodies bowed under ye weight of
> ye same and became decreped in their early youth.

Thus, the Puritans could see the deleterious effects of
work on the quality of life of their children. Just the
same, they persisted in the practice because they
believed in the idea that God wanted all his children to
toil tenaciously on Earth. Clearly, this article of faith
was an ideological fallacy. It put the importance of

---

[4] Abbott, Edith, "A Study of the Early History of Child Labor
in America." *American Journal of Sociology* 14 (July 1908),
at: http://www.boondocksnet.com/labor/cl_0807_abbott.html
In Jim Zwick, ed., *The Campaign to End Child Labor.*
http://www.boondocksnet.com/labor/

preserving an idea, or a set of beliefs, well above avoiding the obvious harms to real persons that resulted from following these beliefs.

In fact, the Puritans saw themselves as expressing positive regard for their children. By compelling the little ones to work hard, the Puritan parents thought they were keeping the children from committing "the sin of idleness."

Attitudes towards child labor shifted away from Puritan righteousness and more towards a callous practicality as the colonies became a new nation with an economy to build. Abbott cites the "Report on Manufactures" written by Secretary of the Treasury Alexander Hamilton in the early 1790's. Hamilton commented that "children are rendered more useful by manufacturing establishments than they otherwise would be."

Hamilton thus expresses a valuation of children that became the rule in American culture. The term "useful" was intended by him to be an expression of positive regard for the children. Indeed, Abbott shows that for the mainstream of American culture, children were valued as useful instruments in the production process long passed Hamilton's day. She notes that "child labor was practically unregulated in this country before the Civil War." But even in states that regulated the hours and wages for children, and compelled attendance at school, the laws "went unenforced." Some factories followed the "family system." Of course, the children were not put in day care, they were put to work. Pregnant women were often used until the day of delivery. While there was some activism by reformist groups after the Civil War, writing in 1908, Abbott observed that child labor has "increased greatly since 1870."

Prior to the Progressive Era of the early 1900's, there were only weak protests against child labor. Men made most of the complaints. They argued that the availability of women and children for low wage labor keeps the pay scales down for them. They demanded that women and children be kept out of the labor market so that men could command higher pay.

Other arguments against child labor were based on the public policy theory that this "national asset" would be more efficiently used if children were compelled to go to school. Then these little "assets" would acquire the "mental and moral improvement ... essential to their becoming ... good [and productive] citizens." We will discuss in a moment why from the point of view of progressive logic the Hamiltonian benign instrumental valuation of children as a "national asset" isn't quite right. But first, let's bring the child labor history up to date.

We saw earlier that abolitionist activists kindled the public opinion that eventually burst into the conflagration of the Civil War. The American public had tolerated slavery for nearly 200 years. But the concerted efforts of passionate reformers, moved by their intuitive sense of progressive logic, agitated the passive mass into motion. Those activists knew their values, and understood that a majority of people shared those values. In the same way, complacent society had done little about child labor until the concerted efforts of progressive activists provoked public opinion into demanding reform.

The "muckrakers" were writers and speakers who forced the public to take notice of the needs for reform in their turn-of-the-century society. Among the leaders of the movement for reforming child labor practices were Edwin Markham, Benjamin B. Lindsey, and George Creel. In the hard-hitting *Children in Bondage*, they wrote:

> Nearly two million! Golden boys and girls -- citizens of the future and mothers that might be -- mangled, mind, body, and soul, and aborted into a maturity robbed of power and promise. They make no cry, these tiny victims. They are too tired. One listens in vain for some bitter wail to ring high and clear above the roar of the machinery that has them in its grasp. ...Amid such unremitting drudgery, such horror of monotony, how can there be talk of health, education, and intelligence? What does life hold out for [these] tiny unfortunate [toilers?][5]

By the early 1900's progressive activists had pressured many states into passing compulsory education laws to keep children in school and out of the factories and fields. Education also became an object of reform, so that it would, as progressive educator Charles W. Dabney said in 1907 "provide opportunities for the development of the whole life of the child." But education reforms were not always effective because some states and local school boards did not implement them. Also, compulsory attendance laws were frequently flaunted and rarely enforced.

---

[5] In Jim Zwick, ed., *The Campaign to End Child Labor*. http://www.boondocksnet.com/labor/ .

No federal law protecting children from the ills of labor existed until progressives pushed through the Keating-Owen Act of 1916. With that law, Congress prohibited the shipment in interstate commerce of any product made by children under 14. This was hardly a comprehensive law. Children had no federal protection if the product was only shipped within a state, and teens 14 and over had no protection under that law. But this was the best progressives could do by way of compromise with the agents of the Robber Barons in Congress.

Two years later, in *Hammer v. Dagenhart*, the Supreme Court declared the law unconstitutional. The opinion stated that Congress had trespassed on the "state's rights" protected by the Tenth Amendment.

Uppity progressives then pressured Congress to pass a second child labor law within a year of the Court's decision. This was the same law, but instead of basing it on Congress's power to regulate interstate commerce, the law imposed a tax of 10% on profits made from child labor. Within a few years, the Court did it again. *Bailey v. Drexel Furniture Co.* held that Congress cannot use taxes as a penalty, only to raise revenue, and that state's rights were violated.

These decisions were designed by our Top Court to allow the captains of industry to use the children of the working class as instruments for multiplying their already outrageous profits. To rationalize these blatant acts of class warfare the Court framed the legal issue as protecting the purity of a juridical concept – state's rights. Protecting this concept was more important to the Honorable Justices than stopping the suffering and slaughter of innocent lives. Just as in *Dred Scott*, the Court revealed its blindness to the ideological fallacy. This value blindness enabled the Robber Barons to use children just as the slave owners used slaves; that is, not as persons but as instruments of production.

The Preamble of the Constitution states that one of the aims of our government is to "promote the General Welfare," and Article One, section 8 vests the power to carry that out in Congress. Clearly, this grant of power was intended by the Framers to be used to enhance the lives of Americans. Certainly, child welfare and public education are essential elements of "the general welfare of the United States." Again committing the ideological fallacy, conservative Supreme Court Justices found more meaning in supporting the airy ideas of "state's rights" and "free enterprise" than in rescuing real children from lives ruined by hard labor.

Finally, among a tidal wave of progressive reforms, the Fair Labor Standards Act of 1938 was passed. It established a set of uniform regulations for the working conditions, hours, and wages of children throughout the United States. Under extreme progressive pressure, the Supreme Court explicitly overruled *Hammer v. Dagenhart* in 1941. *Bailey*, too, has since been discredited.

Today all states have compulsory school attendance laws. In intent, these are ideological enhancements. While some child labor still exists in the U.S., particularly among the urban and rural immigrant populations, state and federal law expresses our country's current understanding of "positive regard" for children. That is, for example, youths under 16 are to be kept out of the work place during school hours. Children under 14 may not work (except, for instance, to deliver newspapers, in entertainment, or for their parents). No dangerous work before age 18. Youths must be paid the minimum wage, and overtime. While states vary, compulsory education is generally from age 6 to 16, and in fourteen states, to age 18.

Considering these laws, has our nation reached its maximum capacity for expressing positive regard for its youth? One often hears the adage that "children are our most precious resource." As we have said, this is an example of our country's predominant benign instrumental valuation of its young people. From the progressive logic point of view, there is a self-contradiction in this way of valuing the young. The valuation of children as "resources" limits their worth to their usefulness; in other words, they are still being valued as things, albeit "precious" things. We will urge below that if all persons always deserve positive regard, then any instrumental valuation of children presents a contradiction.

As an expression of the valuation of youth as precious resources, public education in the U.S. is largely a process for preparing young people to be of use to our socio-economic system. This has proven to be an effective way to enhance the operation of the economy, but are there any adverse consequences for the persons who we put through the process of preparation? In other words, what are the consequences, if any, on the minds of the young people who live in a society that values them as "national resources?" Is each likely to feel that his or her intrinsic worth as a person is being recognized and honored? Or, is each more likely to feel under appreciated, not fully seen, and even somewhat deprecated?

The next wave of progressive education reform will have to address these, and other, questions. In our view, a studied application of progressive logic to the current system of public education shows that the inner dimension of students is being ignored, while all emphasis is on fully developing their production-consumption potential.

For example, as part of their public education experience, students acquire a *personal identity*. Most of that identity is related to the functional needs of the economy. Students learn that education will enable them to develop their "full potential" as producers and consumers. Their personal identity and self-esteem are tied to their role in the economy. The height of wisdom in this ethos is to prepare oneself for a job doing the kind of work you would like to do at the highest pay you can get.

But does this "get and spend" wisdom fully cover the meaning of "a whole life?" Is this wisdom completed if we add, "get a husband," or "get a wife," and "get some kids, so that you have a family to spend your money on?" Is getting and spending unto death the only meaningful way to live a life?

The current meaning of "positive regard" our society is showing its youth is sorely lacking in depth. Instrumental value is shallow, and actually denigrates youth by its faint praise. Some may object that the young are too young to know how they are valued by society. Or, that the way society values them has no effect on their minds. Perhaps they are innocently happy to be processed through an educational system that prepares them for a productive life. But we disagree. While our society no longer forces the young to work in their tender years, our current system of compulsory education does not convey to them that they are valued simply for who they are.

Today, federal spending on public education is barely two cents out of every tax dollar. Nearly twenty cents on the dollar goes for military expenditures. And, eight cents on the dollar is paid out to finance a national debt that did not exist at the beginning of this Century. This budget is the result of a conservative-corporate alliance.

The states, too, are starving the schools. Consequently, and not by accident, many schools are selling classroom time and campus space for kid-directed advertising. Ads for video games and movies packed with destruction, violence, and sexual content, for junk food, gambling, and even tobacco and alcohol are shaping our children's values more effectively than any Health Ed teacher ever could. How's that for treating students as persons?

Young people have value sensors that operate subliminally and register in their minds how society really values them. Much of the malaise, disaffection, rebellion, and self-destructive behavior of "youth culture," especially since the 1950's, is the natural consequence of the way social institutions actually value the young.

Of course, we live in the most complex high-tech society humanity has ever produced. Children need extensive preparation to fully benefit from and contribute to our society. Computer literacy is now as important as are the 3R's. In addition, we live in a republic that aspires to become a democracy. Youth need to know both how much power and how much responsibility they will have as citizens.

But do these educational goals, as noble as they are, fully express to students that they are being valued intrinsically, that is as persons? Or, are these goals no more than the highest refinement of an educational assembly line turning out "good and productive citizens"?

Progressive logic can shed light on these issues, but currently there is no reform agenda around which progressive activists can rally support. What would it take for an institution to fully express to the people who are compelled to pass through it that they are being valued not only as economic operatives in need of preparation, but as persons being educated to fully live "a whole life"? What would be the chief characteristics of a public education system that both compelled minors to attend school, and recognized that each child is a person far more than a potential consumer and producer? Progressives need to plan a full set of "ideological enhancements," or humanizing reforms, by which public education can be made not any less utilitarian, just more student-centered.

Progressive activism is needed to inform and organize parents and civic-minded people to demand an increase in spending on public education, and to insist that commercialism be kept out of the classroom and off campus. Groups like "Commercial Alert," founded by

Gary Ruskin and Ralph Nader to keep commercialism off campus, have the right aims, but often lack public support.

Another way to combat commercialism in schools is to teach students that their happiness need not be dependent upon consumer gratification. Students can be taught to look inwardly to find their own requirements for happiness. To this end, schools should provide youths with an opportunity, and leadership, for developing a stronger sense of self than they now learn in school. The producer-consumer identity can only find meaning in having. But a person with a strong sense of self would be able to determine for himself or herself what forms of meaning are preferable to more having.

Strong self-awareness can be learned in school. This could be done, for example, in adult led small support groups with the singular purpose of exploring and sharing feelings. As one learns to become more aware of, and to express more clearly, one's own feelings, one cultivates a strong sense of self. Such groups could be made a standard part of the four-year high school required curriculum. The groups could meet for one hour a day, two or three times per week. This experience of education through supervised self-reflection and emotionally honest social interaction would enable youths to become fully integrated and self-guiding persons.

A person with a strong sense of self would not need to seek meaning, for example, by identifying with some corporate employer or brand name. A "Chevy girl" or a "Nike guy" necessarily lives a terribly shallow life. But without education as to how to understand oneself, students are only taught to live for having, and to find fulfillment in conspicuous consumption.

America needs a public education system that honors the person passing through it. Such a system would show that person how to become fully in touch with his or her own feelings. Only in this way can graduates learn to live by their own lights. Without a strong sense of self, students are doomed to being distracted by what Kierkegaard called the "mendacious bedazzlement" around them.

As students learn to become more aware of themselves, they also learn that they are worth becoming aware of. In this process, then, each would learn to value himself or herself intrinsically. In addition, this small group experience would also develop every participant's capacity for empathy. Individuals who are out of touch with their own feelings find it difficult to understand that other people have feelings. If other people are only insentient meat, and mere economic automatons, to be valued only for their utility, why should any compassion be given them? A society of individuals with a strong sense of self and a fully developed capacity for empathy would probably use its democratic power for the good of humanity far more than is being done today.

The progressive educational reforms of the past are presently under attack by the Christian right. These conservatives know what they want. That is, "home schooling," "vouchers," an end to compulsory education, and where there are public schools at which their children must attend, they want daily prayers to their "God," and creationism, or "intelligent design," taught as the intellectual equivalent of biology.

They oppose compulsory education laws, saying these laws violate their "liberty." Let's recall the consequences for children when "liberty" was in effect. Factories employed whole families. People in poverty needed the dime-a-day their ten-year-olds could bring home. Children had no childhood, and became "decreped" old people by the age of thirty.

The right wing Christian Family Research Council wants to restore parental power. At least they are honest about what they want. We live in a democratizing society. Our laws often deprive individuals of power over others. Many of the home-schoolers who oppose public education hope to recapture some of that lost power by taking total control over the lives of their children. Their utopia is a Puritan dictatorship of the father over "his" family.

But our society has learned from experience about the need to limit parental power over children. The thrill of using power can easily cloud judgment and cause behavior to exceed reason.

Public education is a measure of the positive regard a society actually has for its youth. Progressives have traditionally advocated an education for the whole person. Sadly, the United States is stifling the development of its youth with a myopic and compulsive focus on career preparation. With this emphasis on the so-called "practical," intellectual development seems secondary. Physical education seems like an optional superficiality. Artistic studies are an "expensive" indulgence. And, the needs for learning empathic social skills and personal development are not even seen.

The U.S. is slowly emerging out of a culture that accepted, indeed profited from, child labor. Notions about the value of youth are changing. How should adults value the young? How should the young value themselves? Public education today is an expression of the pressures between an emerging progressive logic and its conservative resistance. Progressives made significant gains in the first half of the 20th Century. However, that momentum was not carried further in the second half of that Century. Currently reactionary forces are on the rise. Now progressives need a comprehensive reform program that activists will feel like fighting for, so that they can stir the public out of its current paralysis of decision. The room for improvement in public education is as unlimited as is the positive regard our youth deserve.

Children have a variety of needs that public education can fulfill. Among these are the personal developmental needs already discussed. Their physical needs include learning nutrition and how to stay healthy, and sex education. Rigorous exercise in the way of team and individual sports, and self-defense cultivates courage and self-confidence. Schools should provide the opportunity to learn art appreciation, and the techniques of self-expression through such media as painting, drawing, dancing, acting, and singing. To develop their intellects, students need exposure to the full range of human intellectual achievements in history, science, and the humanities. Career preparation is something our schools already do well. Civics education, of course, is crucial to our democratizing society. A well-rounded education has many dimensions.

Standards can be developed in such categories as those mentioned by which to score how well the schools are doing. Within the areas of personal development, physical education, health education, art education, intellectual development, career preparation, and civics, measurable criteria can be specified based on what can reasonably be expected from students by age group and from schools as institutions. Each of these dimensions can be used as a performance standard by which to assess how well schools are meeting the needs of students. The report cards on schools will also be an honest measure of society's positive regard for its youth.

No human institution can be expected to work perfectly. But our public education system, oriented primarily towards job preparation and consumerism, is now failing our youth and our society. At its worst, public education in the U.S. is little more than a system for warehousing instruments of production and consumption until they become useful at the age of 16, 17, or 18. While reforms are needed, we do not need a return to the past. The time for progressive activism is ripe. But activism without ideas is futile; hence, we need both a new agenda and intellectual guidance in forming it.

Progressives need a reform agenda of their own with which to oppose the Christian right. To be authentic, this agenda must be both consistent with progressive logic, and affirm the best of what past progressives have bequeathed us. Progressives can take full credit for establishing the desperately needed reforms of regulating child labor and enacting compulsory education laws. We must build upon these!

Framed in terms of progressive logic, the issue here is how "positive regard" for children should be expressed by our country's child welfare laws and public education institutions. In this new light, new questions will be asked, and new insights will be seen. For example, is home schooling actually an expression of positive regard for children, or more of a personal indulgence for parents who long for that regal power now lost to democratization? (To some extent, this is an empirical question that can be answered by observing the damage, if any, done to children raised by home schooling.) Should school be a job-training center, or a place for personal development? Should students be taught that happiness comes from more having, or comes from self-knowledge?

Compulsory education is still vital to America. Our economic survival depends upon having a population with a uniform minimum level of literacy, and unlimited opportunities for motivated students to attain a higher education. But Americans must learn to expand their understanding of public education to include learning how to enhance one's experience of living. The politics of materialism must now be supplemented with demands for a higher quality of life. Public education can be retooled to meet those demands.

Progressive activists are needed who can lead the public in breaking out of the old mold of valuing the young as resources. There is far more positive regard in valuing youth as persons first. Valuing students as persons means that their personal developmental needs should be fully provided for in public education.

Chapter Three:
Current Life

Work and Community

Karl Marx taught that work is not just the way people make money, it is the way they live. Societies are organized around their own ways of producing, distributing, and consuming the necessities and luxuries of life. American society is far out of balance in each of these dimensions. Our production, distribution, and consumption patterns are resulting in seriously adverse consequences for the environment, for Americans themselves, and for the other people on this planet. Let us consider some of the elements of these three dimensions to our way of life.

Production

Production is the way people work together to produce all the things they need to live in their chosen life style. Marx wrote that humans collectively relate to nature through their production processes. He understood that man evolved out of nature, and turns back to it to sustain his life. Humans relate to nature like no other creature in the history of life. Only humans have a complex system of producing and distributing goods and services based on foresight, planning, planting, intricate tool making, extended education of their young, and with high degrees of cooperation and sharing. The second most social animals on Earth, the primates and four legged predators, are not even close in the degree of complexity and cooperation by which all human groups live. Great apes, like other mammals, care for their young, but when mature the apes live as individuals foraging in groups. They share food even less than do predators, such as lions and wolves. No other mammal has a practice of caring for the sick, wounded, or lame like that of humans.[6]

Clearly, the high degree of cooperation, sharing, and caring for others shows that humans engage in the productive process with a substantial degree of positive regard for one another. However, not all is well. The way we Americans produce, and the things we produce, are now damaging the environment, and if not soon corrected, threaten to cause irreparable harm. We are piling up tons of trash, some of it radioactive. Our manufacturing processes, from cars to computers, cause life-threatening air and water pollution. "Greenhouse gasses" sitting high in the atmosphere are causing global warming. This is changing world weather patterns. Soon, some fertile lands could be turned into deserts, and other fertile land turned into useless arctic tundra. Global warming is causing so much polar ice to melt that coastal cities around the Earth could be flooded. Our agricultural practices are poisoning rivers, lakes, and oceans with a wide range of pesticides, fertilizers, and other toxic chemicals. Traces of those chemicals stay in the food we eat, and once in our bodies, some never leave. Forests all over the world are being decimated to build American mansions, and supply us with mountains of paper (even though computers were supposed to reduce the need for paper). With only 5%

---

[6] See *Good Natured*, by Franz De Waal, and *People of the Lake*, by Richard Leakey.

of the world's population, the U.S. consumes 26% of the Earth's energy.

The human species, like every other form of life, is an extension of the Earth. We are not alien beings that some Higher Power arbitrarily chose to place on this planet. We emerged from processes deeply rooted in nature. Hence, what we do to our Source, we do to ourselves. Our treatment of the Earth, then, is an exact measure of the positive regard that we have for ourselves. Self-destructive behavior is a sure sign that we are not fulfilling our full capacity for the positive regard of ourselves. Hence, the so-called "environmental movement" actually turns on the issue of human self-esteem. The conditions created by man on Earth today manifest excessive self-loathing. A humanity that always holds itself in positive regard would not desecrate that of which it is an extension; i.e., Mother Earth. Thus, to turn our current environmentally destructive practices into environmentally enhancing practices, we must find ways to raise our self-esteem. This can be done. We will show how good laws can help to raise self-esteem in a moment.

Marx had great expectations for what he called "political economy." He anticipated that this "science" would show the way for man to work in harmony with Earth, and for man to work with greater cooperation and respect for one another. Unfortunately, he never completed all the writing on this subject that he wanted to do. But with the guidance of progressive logic to interpret the writings he did leave us, we can see where Marx was headed. Marx, like so many other progressives, unconsciously followed progressive logic. Marx saw that the capitalist-industrial mode of production took the element of community out of human life. That system requires that people on a grand scale value one another as things, or "commodities," or instruments of production, rather than as fellow members of the human community.

Taking our cue from Marx, then, we see progressive logic as leading to the conclusion that work and community should be among the highest priorities on the progressive political agenda. Work and community are the Yin and Yang of society. Ideally, work and community would play an equal and mutually supporting part in enriching the individual's experience of social life. Work would not only aim at producing material goods, but it would be a means of both serving and benefiting from community. We will return to this subject after we consider distribution and consumption.

Distribution

The distribution of the necessities for a decent life in a society is another indicator of the degree of positive regard the people of that society truly have for one another. Actions speak louder than words. In the U.S. today, significant imbalances exist. For example, the total net worth of the United States is about forty-two trillion dollars. The top 1% of the population owns about 33% of that. The middle 49% owns about 64%. The bottom half of the American people own a mere 3% of the nation's total net worth, and close to half of these have actually lost purchasing power in the last twenty-five years.

What do these statistics say about the distribution of positive regard for the people of the United States?

Since our nation's laws structure and preserve our type of economic system, these statistics reflect the government's regard for the people. Government manifests both positive and negative regard for the people through its laws. The shortages of positive regard revealed by the facts of our economy are largely intended by law. The top 1% has its values expressed through our government.

The issues here are very complex. Our society is deeply immersed in the capitalist system. In this historical context, the entrepreneurs who create big and productive businesses may merit a higher share of the nation's wealth. The people who design, market, and sell the products that the workers make may deserve a higher reward, because without them there might be nothing for the workers to do. Thus, some inequality in the distribution of wealth might be more just than a government enforced mathematical equality of dollars per person.

One difficulty for progressive activists, then, is to determine how much inequality of wealth is tolerable, and what degree of inequality becomes an intolerable affront to human dignity. Opinion polls show that Americans at all levels can be very tolerant of some inequality in the distribution of wealth. So, progressives who make the intellectually easy choice of demanding perfect equality of wealth are merely tilting at windmills. That is not going to happen for a long time, if ever. Also, the condition of mathematical equality could not be achieved without a ruthless dictatorship like the one Stalin set up. His government murdered millions to stay in power, and finally bankrupted Russia and the countries it dominated. Few Americans want that to happen here.

Politics is the art of the possible. The history of the labor movement in America is the story of progressive office-holders, activists, and agitators making judgments about what they could possibly achieve in terms of increasing the share of our nation's wealth for the working class. Many important gains were made. The amount of positive regard that U.S. laws showed the people took a huge leap in the first half of the 20th Century. Indeed, the large share of our nation's wealth now held by the middle class was made possible by New Deal reforms brought about by progressive pro-labor activists.

Of course, the material conditions of Americans have changed since the victories of the labor movement were won. Also, the understanding among the people of what constitutes "positive regard" has deepened since then. We will return to this matter in a moment, but first let us discuss consumption.

Consumption

Consumption, rather than community, has become the predominant meaning of life for many, if not most, Americans today. Social status, self-esteem, and the feeling of well-being are tied, in the minds of many, directly to the amount and kinds of possessions they own. These Americans fail to see the importance of community. They are in deep denial of the fact that their chosen way of life robs them of the enrichment to be had in the community experience. Huge numbers of Americans drive to work alone, or keep to themselves on the bus, train, or plane. At work many limit their personal engagements to what is necessary to get the job done. Then they commute home virtually alone. Once home, they turn on the TV, almost as a refuge from life. Within our law-enforced family, many people engage spouse and children on a personal level little more than they do their co-workers.

In large part, this behavior is the natural consequence of valuing oneself and others instrumentally. Because most Americans learn to see themselves as no more than functionaries in the economy, their sensitivities to the intrinsic dimension of value have been numbed. Each person's uniqueness goes unrecognized, and only the common functional elements are acknowledged. Partly out of self-defense, and partly out of self-ignorance, each person creates a façade, or a phony persona, with which to interact with all the others. Tragically, real human contact is very rarely made between persons. "Positive regard" then consists of little more than my persona being courteous to your persona whenever the rules of work or of "society" require it.

Individuals often experience their lives in this situation as lonely, isolated, and empty. But very few understand why they feel this way. Many think that they would feel better if they worked harder or longer and made more money to buy more things. "Perhaps," so their thinking goes, "the prestige of living in a bigger house than do my friends and neighbors, or the power and status of driving a giant gas guzzler, or the bragging rights of taking numerous expensive vacations will help to fill the vacuum."

In 2001 a book came out identifying this condition as a kind of sickness, and labeled it "affluenza."[7] But framed in terms of progressive logic, it can be more precisely called "the instrumental value syndrome." The problem is that people are valuing themselves as things, and not knowing why they feel so incomplete and empty, they seek satisfaction in having more possessions. Its as if each unhappy economic functionary seeks happiness in having his or her own little community of things.

Indeed, we may state as a law of social science that people who value themselves as things seek the company of other things. Hence, pets become "members of the family," and entertainment personalities on the TV screen, in the movies, or in music become, for some, "intimate friends." But animals, sounds, and electronic images are things, not real persons. Consumerism blinds many of us to this glaring distinction. A community of things is not the kind of community we humans really need.

The only way to break out of the instrumental value syndrome is to recognize it, acknowledge it, and to practice seeing yourself and others with more positive regard; that is, as persons. Some people think that the highest form of positive regard for a person is to place him or her on a pedestal and make them into an object of worship, as Americans do with "celebrities." But ask any "celeb" how it feels to be such an object. The honest ones will say it hurts. (See Bob Dylan's autobiography, for example, or the biography of Marilyn Monroe.)

---

[7] *Affluenza: The All Consuming Epidemic*, by John De Graaf, David Wann, and Thomas H. Naylor, 2001

The ultimate value of a person is to see him or her as a unique expression of human life, too precious to be used.[8] And, the only way to fill the emptiness created by the instrumental value syndrome is to be in the presence of people each of whom you see as a person, and each of whom sees you that way, too. That is the ideal condition for fully satisfying one's need for community.

Of course, the ideal often conflicts with the practical. People must work to live, and our highly complex society requires that people use one another as fellow workers, employees, customers, clients, potential buyers to whom a sale can be made if the right words are spoken, etc. Learning to find the balance between the practical needs of work and the ideal way of satisfying the needs for recognition and belonging in a community is one of the greatest challenges facing our society today.

Using the frame of progressive logic can help us to define this problem, and that is a very important start. But only progressive ingenuity and creativity can present the solutions needed. One big question is: What would a political agenda aimed at increasing the degree of community in American life look like?

The beginnings of an answer can be found in the behavior of many Americans today. *Affluenza* cites numerous examples of people quitting their high stress job, and taking big pay cuts at more relaxed work with shorter hours. Many use their increased "free time" to volunteer their services in community action groups. Some people join, or form, "simplicity circles." In these groups people support one another in overcoming their

---

[8] See Martin Buber, *I and Thou*

addiction to stuff. Also, there are thousands of "Twelve Step groups" all across the U.S. These groups focus on common problems such as the traditional Alcoholics Anonymous, Overeaters Anonymous, Co-dependents Anonymous, Adult Children of Alcoholics, Gamblers Anonymous, Credit Card Addicts Anonymous, Cocaine Anonymous, anger management groups, men's groups, women's groups, and more.

Groups are forming around the regular practice of meditation, and the study of spiritual, as opposed to religious, writings. There are even small support groups with the sole purpose of helping one another to get in touch with and express feelings in a non-judgmental setting.

Hardheaded political activists may demand to know "what's all this got to do with politics? Aren't these examples all about personal problems?" The answers are, "no its not about personal problems, its about social problems, and that has everything to do with politics!"

If handled adroitly, the spontaneous support group movement can be parleyed into a mass political movement that will rival the legislative productions of the New Deal. How can this be done? The public needs to know about progressive logic. They also need to understand that their obsession with consumerism is cheating them out of the real riches that can only be had in community. Candidates for office, activists, and agitators can then tell the people that good laws can help them enrich their lives with community.

We need laws that shorten the workday, or the workweek; or, even better, that compel employers to negotiate flexible schedules with all their employees.

Working people deserve much more leisure time, so that they can choose to participate in small groups, go to school, play with their kids, work in the garden, read, or just enjoy life in their own way. Civic centers could provide small group meeting rooms.

Our society has learned from the experiments of the past that government serves the unemployed best when it offers them a hand-up rather than a handout. This policy should be followed to its fullest extent. Experience also shows that people are much happier when they are making a contribution to society by their work than when they are doing nothing on the dole. Opportunities for education, training, and re-training should be greatly expanded so that no person of talent or intelligence will ever be stuck in a dead-end job. More public transportation is needed to reduce time wasted in commuting. Also, vehicle use in urban areas could be regulated to lessen congestion and emissions pollution, as well as to encourage the use of public transportation.

With a system of universal health care enacted by law, both the workers and employers would be relieved of an enormous financial burden. A modest progressive income tax could be enacted to pay for this guaranteed increase in public health. Corporate CEO's are often paid 400 times the pay of their average employees. Isn't it time they gave something back? We also need a Social Security System with a lowered retirement age and payments that seniors can live on.

Progressives who are concerned about the exploited underclass are calling for a "living wage." But the meaning of this term is not the same as a "subsistence wage." A living wage must provide for a decent quality of life. Those wages must be enough to buy the necessities of life on a shortened workweek. Federal law now requires that overtime be paid after 40 hours of work in a week. Why not halve that to 20 hours? With a 20-hour workweek, employers could double the number of people they hire. The money they save from shifting employee health costs over to the federal government could be used to pay the new workers.

Looking at our society through the lenses of progressive logic can help us to see our conditions in a new way. We can see now that American society is on the cusp of a revolution in its understanding of "positive regard." People only need to be shown that laws can be enacted to raise the positive regard that our government extends to them. Once they grasp the idea, nothing will be able to stop them from demanding their just deserts. Let the quality revolution begin!

Abortion and the Right to Die

The Christian right has made the absolute prohibition of abortion its *Holy Grail*. Their obsession is to have *Roe v. Wade*, the 1973 Supreme Court decision, reversed, or to overturn it with a Constitutional Amendment outlawing abortion.

The Supreme Court's finest hour was from 1953 to 1969, when Earl Warren was its Chief Justice. That is when *Brown v. Board* was decided, and a host of rulings were made that honored human worth and dignity. After Warren left the Court, a lack-luster conservative Warren Burger took his place. However, some of the value awareness that Chief Justice Warren brought to the Court carried over to the 1973 decision of *Roe v. Wade*.

That opinion struck down a Texas law banning abortions unless giving birth would endanger the woman's life.

One consequence of this Supreme Court opinion was to begin a dialogue about the meaning of the word "person." The opinion balanced the mother's right of privacy, to consult with her doctor and to obtain medical treatment, against the right to life of a "person" who has not yet been born. A growth in the uterus becomes a person, reasoned the Court, when it has developed into the stage of "viability." That is, when its physiological processes have matured sufficiently to enable it to live independently of the womb. *Roe v. Wade* is a central plank in the progressive agenda, precisely because it defines a key term in progressive logic.

Roe's understanding of a "person" works very well with progressive logic. An embryo is a little container of cells that has no self-consciousness, no sentience, and no memory until its brain has matured enough to produce those functions. Generally, the human brain develops the capacity to carry on these functions after about 26 weeks of pregnancy; or, around the beginning of the third trimester. This is also when the fetus reaches such a degree of viability that it begins to enter into the status of becoming a "person."

The High Court sagely held that in the first trimester a woman and her doctor may freely choose whether or not to have an abortion, without state intervention in the decision. Government may begin to set some regulations restricting an abortion during the second trimester. And, during the third trimester the fetus has a right to life that can only be superseded if further pregnancy or delivery would threaten the life of the mother.

Anti-abortionists screaming "baby killer" at pregnant women entering medical clinics deliberately ignore the science that the Supreme Court studiously relied upon. Brushing aside the subtleties of defining a "person," they arbitrarily proclaim that "life begins at conception." Ignore the facts, they terrorize innocent pregnant women and the doctors and medical staffs who only want to help those women in their time of need. Sometimes these Christian terrorists turn into murderers and kill doctors whom they hypocritically accuse of being "baby killers." Their self-generated feeling of moral superiority enables them to justify their crime, and their supporters honor them as heroes.

As we have mentioned, the Supreme Court was persuaded by science that a non-viable organism is not a "person." Traditionally, the ordinary use of the word "baby" has been in reference to a newborn child. Surviving birth is the surest test of viability. The Supreme Court, then, actually moves the test of viability back to include the third term fetus.

The hysterical Christian right wingers screaming "baby killer" irrationally equate a mindless zygote with a newly born person who has a functioning brain, and a wondering, questioning, inquisitive mind. But their madness is not without method. They are activists and agitators who desire above all to exercise political power for their own ends.

Piety has a long tradition of using moral superiority as an excuse to wield power over other people, and it has never been particular about the validity of its reasoning so long as it helps them to attain power.

Their choice of the "anti-abortion" excuse for grabbing and using political power is based more on political acumen than on rational belief. An intelligent exercise of their will to power has resulted in the calculation that this is a fight they can win.

If the unwanted growth in a woman's uterus is called "cancer," rather than "a baby," conservative strategists would have to concede that they could not organize a political movement with any chance of success based on opposition to the removal of such a cancerous growth. There are Christians who oppose any medical intervention as contrary to "God's will." However, in today's pro-science culture, there simply is not enough material out there with which to shape a movement based on the opposition to all medical interventions. Using astute political judgment, conservative strategists have assessed that public ignorance of science, combined with an ample supply of religious superstition and value confusion, provide them with the opportunity they need to achieve their ends.

Scientifically, abortion is simply a medical procedure for removing an unwanted growth in a woman's uterus. Whether that growth is called "cancer" or "embryo," the quality of the woman's life is just as much at stake. Justice Blackmun displayed great empathy for the pregnant woman when he wrote for the majority in *Roe* that prohibiting all abortions, including very early abortions,

> may force upon the woman a distressful life and

future. Psychological harm may be imminent. Mental and physical health may be taxed by childcare. There is also the distress, for all concerned, associated with the unwanted child, and there is a problem of bringing a child into a family already unable, psychologically and otherwise, to care for it.

Carrying an unwanted pregnancy to term, and then having that helpless infant in one's arms can be a life-altering traumatic experience. This is "her baby." If she keeps her baby, the woman is sentenced to 18 years of unwanted responsibility. If she gives up her baby for adoption, all her mothering and nurturing instincts are frustrated. She risks incurring a lifetime of self-doubt and regret at the lost opportunity to gratify those instincts. This is severe emotional distress that could be avoided by a timely medical procedure.

The idea that all abortions should be prohibited, even if exceptions are made in the cases of rape, incest, and to protect the live of the mother, is an instance of the ideological fallacy. First, it disregards the facts of science in order to preserve itself. (Such as confusing a "baby" with a zygote, blastocyst, or other stage of embryonic development prior to the development of a functioning brain.) Second, as Justice Blackmun observed, it disregards the consequences the idea has on the real persons who find themselves with an unwanted pregnancy.

Roe v. Wade is an instance of an ideological enhancement, because it is based on the premise that the state should express positive regard for the woman in need of an abortion. *Roe* is a law that facilitates the satisfaction of that need, keeping in mind that at some point the fetus becomes entitled to the rights of a person. To make laws intended to frustrate needed medical care is a sadistic act. Laws prohibiting abortion are like laws imposing punishment. They reward the lawmakers and their supporters with the thrills of exercising greater power over those in whom the laws cause suffering. Such laws serve no rational purpose, but only this emotional purpose.

The science-based understanding of a "person," which began to be developed in *Roe*, can be helpful in contexts beyond that of abortion. There are, for example, several important "end of life" public policy problems. If the concept of "viability" entails having a functioning brain with the capacity for self-consciousness, sentience, and memory, then clearly a *dead body* is no longer a "person." (Existing law requires that a corpse be treated with respect, not because it is a "person," but to honor the memory of it in the minds of the living, such as family members.)

When the body is dead, the mind too is gone. But given today's medical technology, the opposite of that proposition is not necessarily true. That is, the mind can be gone, but the body can be kept alive indefinitely by life-supporting machinery. The parts of the brain that produce self-consciousness, primarily in the frontal lobes, can be irrevocably inoperative, i.e. "dead," while the parts of the brain stem that coordinate bodily organs such as heart, lungs, liver, etc. can continue to function if supplied with nutrients.

In cases where the body can be kept indefinitely in a persistent vegetative state, when the brain is dead, there is no longer a viable person. As we have said, viability implies that one's life experience is sustainable by the brain. When the brain has irretrievably lost its capacity to sustain self-consciousness, there is no sentience and no possibility of joy in life. The person is dead. No one is honored by prolonging the functioning of a set of organs in a bag of skin simply because of ethical confusion and the availability of technology.

Hence, laws that provide for a dignified termination of medical life-support systems are fully consistent with progressive logic. The dead person's body should be treated with respect to honor the memory of the person in the living, but not because it is still a person.

The religious idea of the Sixth Commandment, that "Thou shalt not kill," is an instance of the ideological fallacy when applied in these circumstances. First of all Christian hypocrisy bursts out like fireworks on the Fourth of July when they invoke that Commandment to keep brain dead bodies alive. How can people who get tickled by capital punishment, and who rally around the flag with glee whenever there is an excuse for a war be taken seriously when they oppose euthanasia?

Obviously, their opposition to removing brain dead bodies from life-support systems is not based on any consistent application of principle. Rather, that opposition is based on a judgment that this is another political battle they can win. Lacking rational principles, the thrill of winning a battle is their aim. The Bush crowd goofed at this in March of 2005. When they tried to intervene in the case of Terry Schiavo, they ignited such an outcry of public disapproval that they had to back off and let her doctors release her body from its life-support system. There is strong opposition in

American public opinion to politicians using end of life decisions as a political football.

On the other hand, when the brain is functioning and the individual has conscious experience, and may even be able to express himself through blinks or eye movement, although the body is otherwise paralyzed, there is nonetheless still a person. To declare such a person a "non-person," because their body is dysfunctional would be an instance of the ideological fallacy. Terminating the life of such a person would be an act of violence, and an instance of the instrumental fallacy, for violence always reduces the value of a person to that of a thing. Progressive logic holds that the intrinsic value of a *person* is inviolable.

In progressive logic, all such persons always deserve positive regard. Thus, such persons deserve to be taken care of so that they may live as full a life as they can. For someone else to decide that such a person should die from neglect is an act of negative regard, and inconsistent with progressive logic's basic premise. To assure that such persons are accorded the positive regard they deserve, laws are needed that would fully assist the families that care for such members, and that provide for the alternative of institutionalized care. Laws like this would be instances of ideological enhancements on the books, and instrumental enhancements in practice.

Positive regard requires that the lives of persons be protected by law. But there is another implication of positive regard. That is that every living person has a right to die with dignity. This includes the right to decide to die at a time of their own choosing. A person may be in great pain, which medicine tragically may be unable to alleviate or heal. Positive regard for a person in such a condition would respect their decision to either stay alive and endure their pain, or to end the pain by dying. No one should be compelled by law to continue suffering against his or her will.

Because progressive logic requires that the capacity for reason in people be honored, a person's decision to die, if taken out of reason rather than despair, deserves to be honored. Allowing death with dignity honors the living person. He or she is given the choice of how and when to die. Blanket prohibitions on euthanasia subject the living person to someone else's ideas about what is right and wrong for him or her. Such rules are callous notions and rigid formulas that deny rational people the opportunity to make distinctions between cases and to make free decisions in varying circumstances as to what is best for the living person.

Laws that flatly prohibit doctor-assisted suicide and euthanasia are instances of the ideological fallacy. They place the intellectual purity of not taking a life above the actual person whose life is being consumed by unendurable pain. Such "purity" by lawmakers is pure hypocrisy. Governments justify killing people for all sorts of reasons. Many states exercise capital punishment with relish. In the time George Bush II was governor of Texas he permitted 103 executions! Yet, he opposes stem cell research on the pretense of respect for human life! All governments allow police and citizens to kill in self-defense, and in the defense of another person. Deadly force can even be used to stop the commission of a felony theft of property, or to stop an escaping felon in some circumstances. All governments celebrate killing in war. No government is in a moral position to deny the right to die.

For the law to compel a suffering person to continue suffering against their will has the same result as torture. Government sanctioned torture inflicts pain on a person against his or her will. As violence, it is an instance of the instrumental fallacy. It uses a person as a thing. Those "ideologically pure" laws, which command that suffering be allowed to continue, even while the power to stop the pain is right at hand, display a callous and negative regard for the person. In both cases, the state is responsible for the continuing pain of the person. Laws prohibiting torture show positive regard for the person. Laws allowing euthanasia and death with dignity should be enacted for the same reason.

Should the state allow suicide? To outlaw suicide is an absurdity. One purpose of law is to regulate behavior through the use of corrective rehabilitation. Another purpose of law is to punish violators, whether to compel them to correct their behavior or as an example to others. But if a person kills himself, there is no one left to either rehabilitate or to punish! Such laws are useless.

Laws permitting suicide, or having no law on the matter, would show more positive regard for the individual than do laws prohibiting suicide. Government shows positive regard for individuals when it respects their decision whether to live or die. However, empathy makes clear that human beings are apt to see death as the only way out of problems, pain, or hardships when in fact there may be less drastic options.

Hence, some form of protecting people in despair from ill-advisedly rushing into self-destruction should be put into law. For example, psychologists who specialize in consulting people with self-destructive impulses should be made easily accessible to the public, in hospitals and clinics.[9] "Suicide hot-lines" are already available for people in despair to talk to a sympathetic person. Such services need more public funding.

The lines between killing as violence, and killing as an act of mercy and compassion, as well as when to facilitate and when to discourage suicide, are not subject to simple-minded purity. Laws that are enhancements in such situations would guide doctors and hospitals in taking the decision whether to assist a suffering person's suicide, or to engage in euthanasia. People in the helping professions need laws that give them guidance in making end of life decisions. Lawmakers, working with professional organizations and interested members of the public, are perfectly capable of enacting procedures for end of life decisions that would insure both due process of law and positive regard for those for whom death is the best option.

The Conservative Mentality

Surely, all progressives can agree that we need to increase the number of votes cast for our candidates in

---

[9] Psychologists should be allowed to write prescriptions for medications that are relevant to their practice. Too often access to needed medicine is burdened by limiting the right to write prescriptions to medical doctors. MD's often lack the professionally trained empathy and understanding that doctors of psychology have. More positive regard would be shown for clients if they could obtain the medications they need from their therapist, rather than having to endure the humiliation of going begging to doctors.

elections, and for our legislation in Congress. For conservatives to continue prevailing in these matters is intolerable. Fortunately, this situation can be turned around. To defeat the conservatives, we must first understand how they sustain their position. This will help to reveal their more vulnerable points. We know that conservatives maintain their predominance by appealing to the minds of millions of American voters. To undercut that appeal, we must understand how it works. In short, conservatives stay in power by satisfying certain needs in their supporters. By shedding light on the demand/supply relationship between the conservative leadership and their supporters we progressives will be able to find ways to cut some of those connections.

Friedrich Nietzsche, the late 19th Century German philosopher, is a leader in the psychological study of why people crave power. In *Beyond Good and Evil* [10] he observes that moral ideologies are simply instruments for acquiring power. Many, if not all, human minds have within them a "will to power," according to Nietzsche. This moves people to seek political power. The apex of this power is, of course, the capacity to control the lives of others, to inflict pain, and ultimately, to kill with impunity.

Writing before Freud, who has acknowledged Nietzsche's influence on him, Nietzsche saw that satisfying this will to power could provide people with strong emotional gratification. Supporters of political leaders are rewarded at the deepest level by the vicarious satisfaction of their individual wills to power. To see their leaders exercising political power can

---

[10] Also see his essay, "*The Genealogy of Morals.*"

provide masses of people with both the thrill of victory and with a sadistic pleasure. Many people are quite willing to make individual sacrifices for the joys of being on the winning side. Indeed, experiencing the vicarious pleasures of using political power can become the highest purpose of their lives.

Another well-known philosopher, Bertrand Russell, wrote in a book entitled *Unpopular Essays*, that intense emotional gratification can be had by people who identify themselves as "morally superior" to others. Those who feel like victims often claim such "moral superiority." This feeling can help compensate for the resentment and pain people often experience when they perceive themselves as having been deprived of some material or political advantage.

Religious organizations can exploit these bitter feelings by inducing a sense of moral superiority in their supporting membership. Making their members feel that they have a "special relationship" with their "God," also helps to both expand and to shore up their base. People who believe they have such a special relationship feel less fear of "The Almighty." They also feel that their special alliance with The Almighty bolsters their imaginary power against those whom they define as "out groups," like secular progressives.

Throughout history religious demagogues have used these marketing techniques to build their base. They have been especially successful at it in the U.S. since the 1980's and the "Reagan Revolution." The demagogues use electoral victories to confirm to their supporters that "God is on our side." Their followers also enjoy the vicarious thrill of "team victories" from winning elections. The election and re-election of

George Bush II has enabled "born again" Christians to find a complete validation of their special relationship with "God." By imagining that "Jesus helped" in these elections, right-wingers can provide themselves with "proof" of their moral superiority and specialness.

With victory come the spoils. For these "Christian soldiers," the spoils come in the form of emotionally gratifying laws and symbols. George Bush II has given them a nice little war in Iraq to rally around and to draw vicarious thrills from. They are getting laws that limit and burden a woman's right to an abortion, and a Supreme Court that is itching to reverse *Roe v. Wade*. They have the pleasure of seeing more people in U.S. prisons than in any other five industrial nations combined. Their desire to see a stream of prisoners executed by the government under the laws of capital punishment is being thoroughly satisfied. In several states they are getting "home schooling" laws that exempt their kids from public education. They are getting their kicks from seeing laws enacted that reduce federal expenditures for programs that feed kids hot breakfasts, school lunches, and that present educational shows to children on public television.

Congress and the president are giving their conservative supporters a federal bench that is chock-full of their kind. Republicans have a "court-packing plan" that would astonish even FDR by its boldness, and make him envious by its success. Everyone knows that overturning *Roe* is the ultimate aim of their court-packing scheme, and they do not deny it. The Supreme Court is bending over backwards (or should we say forwards?) for them. Despite the original intention of our Constitution's Framers to separate church and state the Supreme Court is stretching credulity in every way possible to keep the conservatives happy. When the symbols of Christianity, such as the cross, the Ten Commandments, the nativity scene, etc. are displayed on government grounds, in public buildings, or in other public places, the desired effect is to associate Christian moral superiority with the governmental power of the United States.   Recently the Supreme Court has approved a huge granite monument displaying the Ten Commandments in front of a Texas courthouse.

Conservatives are willing to accept symbolic substitutes for real positive regard. Governments can extend actual positive regard for its citizens through laws and policies that enrich their lives. Laws enforcing civil rights, like laws enacting universal health care or providing for fair elections, are examples of how government can express positive regard for its people. But rather than demand authentic expressions of positive regard from their political leadership, conservatives feed off symbolic measures that confirm their specialness in the Eyes of God, the moral superiority of their religion, and that provide the sadistic pleasure they derive from denying good laws to others.

The genius of the conservative strategists since Reagan's election has been to associate the symbols of Christian moral superiority with the political agenda of the Republican Party's corporate right wing. In reality, there is no intellectually defensible connection between the increase of corporate control over American society, and the world economy, and the principles of Christianity. But millions of voters have been induced into voting to support corporate power by the Christian bait offered to them.

In return for their vote, they do *not* get economic policies that are in their best interest; indeed, for years they have been losing purchasing power, job security, health care benefits, and retirement security. They are being forced to live in a media environment that deliberately targets their children for brain washing into consumerism. Ironically, many of them resent and denounce the values of consumerism even as they vote into office the puppets of the masters of consumerism.

Baffled and outraged progressives often fail to understand that these Christian conservative voters are not stupid, nor naïve, nor are they alien invaders from "Dumbfuckistan." Conservative political activity conforms perfectly to the explanatory model that we use to help make sense of human behavior. That is, that human behavior tends to be preceded by a plan for, or an expectation of, some sentient benefit. This is the model of "plan, act, and enjoy." Many of our conservative opponents are rational, in fact heroic, actors. They know their values. They have arranged their priorities. They have calculated how best to get what they want. And, they are willing to work hard and to make economic sacrifices to win the symbolic victories they seek and to enjoy the pleasures they desire.

Progressives who only see the materialistic stupidity of the low-income right are like the old generals who are still fighting the last war. Hey guys, the labor movement is long gone! The right is fighting for the quality of life that they want to experience. Largely because they know what they want, and the left does not know what it wants, the right is winning. Their ultimate aim is to make a "Christianocracy" of America, and they just might do that.

United and effective progressive activism is the only way to stop this Christian extremist march towards hell. So, let us look more closely at the motives and successes of the right. Then we will be better able to gauge their vulnerabilities, and to plan our method of attack.

Chapter Four:
The Crime of Punishment

Christian Justice

A prime example of extremist Christian power over American institutions is the criminal justice system. From the progressive logic point of view, the criminal justice system in the U.S. is a model of Christianocracy at work. Progressives have made substantial and lasting improvements in several areas of our society. Slavery was abolished, women have gained equality, worker rights have been instituted, public education established, and civil rights are firmly in place and enforced by the courts. But progressive efforts at reforming the criminal justice system have made little headway since our country became an independent nation.

Why is that? What social function does the criminal justice system fulfill that renders it so immune to reform? Anyway, why would anyone want to reform that system? Doesn't it protect society from crime?

With the elements of progressive logic now articulated, the fair minded person will be able to see more clearly than ever before why the American criminal justice system is unacceptable as an institution in the United States. We will show below how the system functions, and why it has been so resistant to change. The bright light of progressive logic will reveal a mean, sadistic system. Our logic will reveal that the system's supporters lie about its intended purposes of public safety and the rehabilitation of offenders so as to effect goals that require widespread psychological denial.

Most of what we write here is an elaboration upon the insights of America's premier champion of criminal justice system reform, Karl Menninger. In *The Crime of Punishment*, Menninger states a comprehensive critique of the American criminal justice system. He chronicles numerous suggestions for reform that have, with little success, been urged upon the people of the U.S. We will take what Menninger has written, and reframe it in the terms of progressive logic. This new frame will empower us to clarify the value transgressions of the system. We will also build upon Menninger's discussion of proposed reforms, and offer an outline of a system that is true to the aims of public safety and the rehabilitation of offenders. Armed with the knowledge of progressive logic, we progressives may be able to leverage enough public support to force monumental change onto this medieval system.

America's criminal justice system follows our model of action; that is, plan, act, and enjoy. A "plan" need not be a detailed blueprint, or a charter with clauses and sub-clauses. Like the English constitution, it can be a generally understood set of customs, even while not explicitly stated. Indeed, public support for our criminal justice system rests heavily upon its plan *not* being stated. So long as the functional intent of the system is kept in the shadows, no one will have to acknowledge what they are being a party to. For, if the mirror of Truth were shown to them, most would turn away in shame. Hence, merely stating what functions the system fulfills will be the beginning of its end. Few Americans would consciously continue to do what they are now unconsciously doing with that system. Our message to progressive activists, then, is to go out and make the unconscious conscious. But we will return to this matter of practical politics after we have presented our understanding of the criminal justice system, and suggested an alternative to it.

The American criminal justice system has roots running deep into a European past. In the Dark Ages, when the Catholic Church dominated most of Europe, criminal justice customs that long predated the Church were selectively adopted, blessed, and given reason in the Bible.

As kings emerged to become equal powers with cardinals and bishops, royal courtiers devised a new idea for criminal justice. The "divine right" of kings to carryout "God's will" through the law helped to solidify secular power against the Church. To help secure their conquest of England in 1066, the Normans shrewdly devised the jury system. That gave the people a share in the power to determine the guilt or innocence, and the punishment, of persons accused of committing a crime. The ancient practice of trial by combat gave way to the use of articulate representatives to plead one's case when circuit judges came to town.

In the 1600's, English colonists brought their long-standing legal customs with them to America. Despite much hullabaloo about reform over the years, since the birth of the United States, the reform of the criminal justice system has been itsy-bitsy at best. Complex criminal codes define procedures that confound the brightest of lawyers. Appellate courts work daily at trying to explain these unexplainable procedural rules. The criminal codes deliberately baffle the public so as to ward off their attention, and reserve the domain of code writing and interpretation to the lawyers. These codes help preserve the worst features of the criminal justice system. That is one reason why arrest and trial procedures, which can lead to prison and execution, are still the system's essence. Blocks of gated cells encircled by barbed wire, or razor wire, and guarded by armed men are an enduring characteristic of American prisons.

As in the past, executions by the dozens are carried out annually with the only "reform" being the use of lethal injection rather than firing squad, hanging, or electrocution. (Marxists would say that this reform pattern parallels the rise of pharmaceutical corporations over the once powerful electric utility companies.) Of course, the result for the condemned person is always the same; a premature demise brought about by his fellow man, and at taxpayer expense.

Least changed of all is the adversary system. That is, the practice of dueling lawyers saying whatever they can get away with before judge and jury to win that contest called a "trial." The prisoner's fate is used as the reward for the winner in the adversary system. The District Attorney, employed by the state, is the winner if the accused is convicted. The defense attorney, often a Public Defender, is the winner if the accused is acquitted. Studies have long shown that if the defense attorney is a highly paid hired gun in private practice, the accused has a much better chance of acquittal than if he is represented by an overworked Public Defender. In any case, Winning, not Truth or Justice, is the object of both sides.

A District Attorney who can rack up a lot of convictions gains an edge if he has political ambitions. Successful DAs often go on to higher elected office. Voters are impressed by high conviction rates. No Public Defender can base a political campaign on how many acquittals he has won. The public would see that as being soft on crime. Indeed, public opinion about crime and punishment is the ultimate basis of the American criminal justice system, and the main reason why that system has changed so little.

Karl Menninger spent much of his professional life as a psychiatrist, criminologist, expert witness, and consultant to governments and law reform commissions. He had a strong sense of progressive values, and long advocated reform of the criminal justice system. He also saw the psychological function the system served for the public. *The Crime of Punishment* is a study of American social psychology, as well as a call for reform. In the following pages, we will first review Menninger's vision of the symbolic function that the criminal justice system has for the American psyche. Then we will draw from his recommendations for reform, and outline an alternative process for assuring the public safety and for rehabilitating offenders.

The U.S. criminal justice system plays a special role in the American mind. According to Menninger, Americans relate to that system above all as an audience to a "morality play."[11] For many Americans, this drama both reaffirms deep-seated religious values and satisfies several unconscious desires. Crime news in the media is "a kind of sermon." [12] It keeps alive the basic lesson of the Old Testament. That is, that those who do forbidden deeds will face the wrath of a righteous Higher Power.

---

[11] P. 154.
[12] P. 154.

Old Testament essays are full of this moral lesson. Eat the forbidden fruit, look where you are told not to look, have too much fun, and a vengeful God will drive you from Paradise, turn you into a block of salt, or flood the whole planet.

Members of the audience identify in various ways with the protagonists in the drama; the police, judges, and criminals. The authorities of the criminal justice system are like the representatives of God, carrying out His will on Earth. One of the symbolic functions of the criminals is to become "the embodiment of all evil."[13] News of the police arresting one of the "evildoers," or of a judge sentencing one to a stiff term in state prison, reaffirms the worldview of the Christian right's most important text. Such news lends validity to the Biblical prophecy that in the end, the allies of God will be saved, and all the evildoers condemned to perdition. Indeed, for some, the very existence of God seems to be "proven" every time good prevails over evil. In a society turned uncertain by science, the hunger for such "proof" is insatiable.

American social thinkers have provided no convincing alternative worldview to this Biblical story of a vengeful Higher Power pursuing the evil ones. Indeed, the entertainment industry has made billions of dollars by replicating this one theme in tens of thousands of movies, video games, and TV shows. Hence, moderates, and even liberal Christians, as well as non-Christians are conceptually unprepared to see the criminal justice system out of this morality play frame. But before we show how to see the system differently, let us elaborate on the implications of Doctor Menninger's analysis.

---

[13] P. 9.

For, this morality play has other functions than sermonizing and providing amusement. It also provides a pleasure that gives meaning to the lives of millions of Americans; namely, those who live for the vicarious thrills of vengeance.

In the realm of the unconscious, logic holds little sway. Thus, members of the public may identify with the authorities in the criminal justice system as their "official avengers,"[14] but they may also identify with some of the criminals, too. The wily crooks and gangsters who succeed, like The Godfather, as well as the bold actors, even if brought down, like Bonnie and Clyde and Billy the Kid, are made into folk heroes. The morality play has such versatility that the same people can derive a vicarious thrill from identifying with the "cops" one moment, and with the "robbers" the next.

Some of those who derive a secret joy from the news of criminal acts may then carry a load of guilt for their "bad thoughts." Then the attraction of crime reports turn into a symbolic self-punishment as they identify with the victim! For others, every report of a crime is an opportunity to indulge in moral superiority. With each "tisk-tisk" they wallow in the self-assurance that the vengeful God is their ally, because they are so "good."

"Goodness," itself is defined not in the least by humanitarian standards, but only by one's alliance with the Supreme Being. "Good" is that which God, through the Bible, has said it is. Of course, the All Mighty is unconstrained by any such man-made notion as the progressive premise that all persons always deserve positive regard. The Old Testament God is a war lord,

---

[14] P. 144.

generous to His allies, but capable of heartless cruelty and murder against His enemies – the disobedient and the non-believers.

This is a scary God. His most devout followers are moved primarily by the vicarious titillation of the will to power that their allegiance gives them. They want to tweak the power pleasure centers of their brains by identifying with an imaginary Super Action Hero. The less devout ally themselves with this version of the Christian God as an insurance policy. They are mostly concerned about assuaging their fear of the unknown. The psychic pleasures that the morality play provides for the public, plus the lack of any conceptual alternative, is the main reason that the system persists.

Menninger's analysis clearly shows that the main pillar of the American criminal justice system is this country's cult of vengeance. This cult consists of individuals, numbered in the millions, with a common addiction to the power pleasures that the criminal justice system supplies. Knowing of the punishment of offenders is the primary source of this pleasure. Many Americans believe in the Old Testament theory that punishment should be given those who do what has been forbidden, and prisons are the place where that punishment is carried out. Prisons operate as Americans want them to operate; that is, as institutions in which inmates will live monotonous and stressful lives. Because prisoners live in fear of one another and of their guards, they are deprived of normal social relationships. They are deprived of normal sexual contacts. They are compelled to engage in meaningless labor, and they are unprepared for a normal life once released. Menninger observes that "we all know how miserable prisons are. We want them to be that way."

Menninger wrote optimistically in the 1960's about the prospects for future reform in prison management. However, recent trends have gone the other way. As the Christian right has ascended to power in American politics, they have forcefully tightened the screws on the prison population. Menninger anticipated that human innovation would produce new ways of rehabilitating those convicted of severe anti-social behavior. Writing at the end of the Warren Court era, he naively assumed that humane feeling was on the rise in the U.S. He thought that the public would overcome its addiction to the pleasures of punishing their brothers and sisters, and find ways to redeem the lives of offenders. But the Warren era was an anomaly in Supreme Court history, and not indicative of a lasting trend in American public opinion.

Instead of increased humanity, American ingenuity devised the "three strikes" law. The voters in the state of Washington passed the first three strikes initiative in 1993. California, often thought of as a progressive state, passed its three strikes law, Proposition 184, in 1994. The vote was 72% to 28%; in other words, the measure easily passed by nearly a three to one margin. By 2004, 26 states and the federal government had some version of that law.

The law provides that after any third felony conviction, the evil one can be confined in prison for life. It does not matter how long ago the first two convictions were, they will still be counted against you. Even if your priors were committed as a juvenile, and you lived a straight life for a quarter of a century, or a half a century, one more slip up and off you go!

In California, third convictions leading to a life sentence have been based on such horrendous crimes as stealing golf clubs, shoplifting some videotapes, and boosting a pizza. Of course, these cases were taken to the Supreme Court. Surely the Eighth Amendment's prohibition of cruel and unusual punishment would apply here. But under the leadership of conservative Chief Justice William Rehnquist, the High Court bent over once again to please the Christian right. In the 2003 decisions of *Ewing v. California* (golf clubs), and *Lockyer v. Andrade* (videotapes) the Court saw no violation of the Eighth Amendment, and upheld the sentences.

A coalition of outraged moderates and progressives in California managed to put Proposition 66 on the 2004 ballot. This modest adjustment of the three strikes law would require that the third strike be "serious" and/or "violent." But the Christian right would have none of it. They pumped out reams of propaganda against "coddling criminals," paid for by their corporate allies. Over five and a half million voters cast a "yes" vote on the matter. Sadly, 6.2 million voters said "no."

California voters are serious about the pleasures they get from punishment. As if a life sentence was not enough for stealing golf clubs, videotapes, or pizza, they also demanded that all the weight lifting equipment be removed from the state prisons. They got their way. In fact, Arizona was the first state to devise this additional torture. Delighted with the idea, California and several other states soon followed. As a result of these Christianocracy measures, the recidivism rate among "third strikers" has dropped to zero, but there has been a substantial increase in their rates of suicide.

Deterrence Theory

Voices from the cult of vengeance may vociferously object that such tough action deters crime, and that the whining liberals are insensitive to the feelings of those whom the criminals have victimized. Blinded by their addiction to punishment, these cultists fail to see the facts in both instances.

First, no victims of crime are turned into happy campers by the punishment of the offender. Ask any victim of rape if she or he has been made happy by knowing that the rapist received five or ten years in prison for his brutality. Ask any mother, father, relative, friend, or lover of a murder victim if they have been restored to wholeness by the execution of the murderer who caused their loss.

Punishment doesn't pay. The victims never get back what they have lost simply because the offender has been punished. Only the on-looking unvictimized public can find any pay-off in punishment.

Secondly, Menninger rejects the so-called "deterrence theory" of punishment. The behaviorist theory dominates in criminology. It says that punishment conditions offenders to not engage in acts that will get them punished again. As evidence, they have stacks of studies showing how laboratory dogs, cats, and rats have been conditioned by electric shocks not to drink from the cup on the left of their cages, but only from the cup on the right. However, no matter how much fun the behaviorists have with their corporate funded experiments, their theories simply do not apply to people.

In reality, people commit crimes for many reasons. Often crimes are the result of impulses that the actor can neither understand nor control. Past punishments and the prospect of future punishment do not affect such impulses. Sometimes crimes are committed by folks with risk taking personalities who calculate that they will not be caught. Indeed, the system entices risk takers, because most crimes go unreported or unsolved, and most arrests do not result in convictions. These factors move first time offenders, second time offenders, and career criminals no matter what their punishment history may be. These enticements are an essential element of the system.

High recidivism rates show that punishment, without rehabilitation, of offenders has little deterrent effect. Punishment often produces people whose second crimes were worse than the first. Jails frequently turn out smarter, bolder crooks that have learned how to commit crimes without getting caught again.

Behavioral deterrence theory is not science, but mythology used by the cult of vengeance as ideological justification. As Menninger notes, "the deterrence theory is used widely as a cloak for vengeance."[15]

Educating Human Sensitivity

Our society's interpretation of the Old Testament eye-for-an-eye theory of justice is a tempered version of the

---

[15] P. 206.

one followed in medieval Europe. Torture was as prevalent then as crime shows are on TV today. Life was so cheap that poor beggar children caught stealing bread could have their bones broken on a machine called "the rack." Offenders then could have each of their limbs tied to one of four horses. Then the riders would have a contest to see which limb would remain attached the longest. The winner would drag the limb and groaning torso through the crowd to spark their sadistic joy.

These contests, plus lynchings and burnings were conducted as ritual festivals throughout Catholic Europe. Such exhibitions were like the carnival coming to town. Families would pack a picnic lunch. There were troubadours, jugglers, and clowns. Everyone felt thrilled at hearing the agonized screams of the evil ones. Far from humanizing these barbaric practices, the Church itself conducted public burnings of witches, heretics, and homosexuals for the fun of its flock.

Human sensitivity to the suffering of others was not educated by religion in Europe, but by the rise of science. Medical treatment, for example, became increasingly humane, and more effective, as doctors began seeing patients as physically ill rather than as possessed by the devil or other evil spirit. Psychology followed the same pattern. Crazy people in the streets were either brutalized by a laughing public, or confined to dungeons kept by sadists. With the rise of science, the idea of "mental illness" became accepted, and treatment began to replace torture.

Believe it or not, even the criminal law of England became a little more humane with the rise of science.

English judges invented the "M'Naughten rule." This placed some limitations on the number of people the law could order executed. If, in the opinion of science, the accused was so insane at the time of the crime that he could not tell the difference between right and wrong, then he should be spared the death penalty.

The scientific worldview has measurably humanized humanity. It continues to do so. In the United States, scientific studies have provided support for several progressive reform movements. Social science studies, and medical studies, have been used by progressive activists to convince the American public to push for all sorts of reforms. These include regulating the work place for children and adults, instituting public education, enforcing public sanitation laws, and making improvements in hospitals for both the physically and the mentally ill. Only the criminal justice system has proven to be immune to the rise of science-inspired humanization of public institutions.

Menninger's analysis of the American mind has shown us why there has been so little humanization of the criminal justice system. Modern prisons are the remnants of "medieval torture dungeons."[16] The pleasure Americans take from our system of punishment lines us up "with the Marquise de Sade."[17] Based upon his decades of study and experience, Menninger writes that the "inescapable conclusion is that society secretly *wants* crime, *needs* crime, and gains definite satisfactions from the present mishandling of it!"[18]

---

[16] P. 131.
[17] P. 210.
[18] P. 153, emphasis in original.

Real, rather than behavioral, social science shows that the majority of those who are punished by imprisonment come from the lower echelons of society. This is where the high school drop out rates may exceed half the enrollment. Economic frustration and emotional confusion is higher here. Violence is far more common among the poor than among the middle class and the rich. Mental illness is far less likely to be treated here, as is illness generally. Ignorance about nutrition combined with high drug use exacerbates mental and physical illness, crime, and violence. Arrest rates are highest among the poor, and their ability to make bail or to hire defense counsel is the lowest of all the economic classes.

Crime holds out the temptation to make big money quickly. The alternative is degrading work at paltry wages. In other words, poverty pressures people to engage in crime. Most people resist the temptation, but enough succumb to keep the system well fueled. Hence, the elements of the criminal justice system include far more than the police, courts, and prisons. The process as a whole also entails poverty to produce criminals and, of course, the news media to report all the goings on.

All of this is well known, and has been well known for many decades. Yet, nothing is done to change the conditions that predictably produce the bulk of the criminals. Menninger explains why. The public both needs and uses the bottom class to produce players for the drama. As we have said, the function of poverty as a supplier of criminals is essential to the existence of the criminal justice system. While the voters love the punishment of the convicted, few people realize that, as Menninger writes, "the prevalent punitive attitude of the public toward criminals is self-destructive."[19] As he understood, a system that produces criminals necessarily also creates victims, and no one knows who the next victim will be. However, the police confine most of the violent crime to the poorer areas, so the rich and middle class folks feel that the risks of maintaining the system are worth the rewards they derive from it.

The benefits to the public also extend beyond the mere news of cops, robbers, and the misery of prison life. Everything included, the system validates the Christian worldview. It provides visible evidence for the belief in the existence of "good and evil." The true believer can almost see the invisible hand of their vengeful God influencing human events as the police nab the evil ones on the street. If the principle of "plan, act, and enjoy" can explain any human behavior, then it explains what we have here; in other words, a set of man-made social processes which resist reform because of the pleasurable meanings they produce for the majority of voters.

Thanks to the groundwork laid by Menninger, we can now see even deeper into these inhumane processes, and realize that the criminal justice system is of itself an establishment of religion. It is a massive, blatant, and unchallenged violation of the First Amendment's explicit prohibition against government making laws "respecting an establishment of religion."

Christianity would have little political influence in America without the criminal justice system and its auxiliary feeding mechanism, poverty, to make the Christian ideology seem real. Without the criminal justice system continuously teaching and validating the

---

[19] P. 156.

Old Testament theory of "justice," right wing Christianity would lose its very sustenance. Rich preachers would lose their easy incomes. The corporations would lose their voting block. DAs would no longer get elected to higher office. Trial lawyers would have to find honest work. Without its allies among the conservative Christians, the Republican Party would collapse to the size of a special interest group for the superrich. Sustaining the criminal justice system is vital to the life of the right. But that system is also their Achilles' Heel.

Progressive Justice

Progressive logic shows the value contradictions in the American criminal justice system. As we have seen, that system is based primarily on the Biblical idea of "justice;" that is, that one who has done a forbidden act must be punished. Sustaining this religious idea of justice is the aim of the voters in the cult of vengeance. That idea is far more important to them than is any concern they may have for the suffering of the evil ones, our brothers and sisters, who are punished within the system. Despite their phony protestations to the contrary, these pious Christian extremists are really not concerned about the plight of the victims that the criminal justice system feeds on. The Christian right votes in ways that sustain poverty, even though they are also trapped within it. But they are not fools, they willingly pay the price for the power pleasures they receive. They want society organized *by this design*, because the results are so yummy.

Here, of course, is the ideological fallacy. The idea is

regarded as more important than the persons who are made to suffer to sustain the idea. Indeed, both criminals and victims are the human sacrifices our Christianocracy offers to its vengeful God. However, for progressive logic, the quality of human lives is infinitely more important than preserving a self-destructive system. If all persons always deserve positive regard, then ideas should enhance the human experience, not detract from it.

Within the operation of this system, the instrumental fallacy occurs in tens of thousands of instances everyday. Both criminal and victim are valued instrumentally as the feedstock without which the system could not function. But if all persons always deserve positive regard, then they should never be used as mere means to satisfy sadistic lust and to validate religious fanaticism.

Progressive logic's basic premise, that all persons always deserve positive regard, was the key principle of value that drove the abolitionists to push the public to put an end to slavery. The same principle provided the impetus to the progressive activists who prodded the public to end child labor and to institute public education. Activists, moved by the same value principle, succeeded in gaining enough public support to improve the conditions of adult workers, and to achieve respect and equal rights and civil liberties for women and for all non-whites. Here, then, is the reason to remove the criminal justice system, and to replace it with a more humane and effective system of protecting the public from crime and of rehabilitating offenders.

Over one hundred years ago, progressives were the first people in American history to advocate seeing social problems from the public health point of view. This is the view of science. The amazing progress in the history of medicine and psychology shows that when educated people cleanse from their vision the obscuring lenses of the belief in "sin" and "evil," they see a world that is amenable to practical problem solving. Science teaches people to think descriptively about processes, rather than judgmentally about behavior. "Sin" and "evil" hide behind a mystical aura of "eternal truths," thus discouraging change. As we have seen, powerful groups of people in the U.S. benefit from perpetuating such muddled thought. But an education of the public by progressive activists could change the way a sufficient number of voters think so that the cancer of Christianocracy can be cut from the body politic, letting a humane healing take its place.

Menninger mentions numerous examples of progressive ideas for a public health alternative to the present criminal justice system. Drawing from these notions, we now suggest the following outline for a new "Public Safety System" to replace the current governmental establishment of Old Testament Christian justice. If public safety, and not sadistic pleasure and the validation of religious myths, is our one and only true purpose, then the way is clear. We need a system with but two functions. One is to take offenders into official custody. The other is to determine what they need to help them to become healed prior to release.

A crime need not be seen as a "sin," or an act of "evil." Crimes can be seen as a cry for help from a forlorn soul, frustrated, angry, in deep pain, and without self-understanding or self-control. Many crimes are the expression of such helplessness and despair. One aim of the Public Safety System would be to take these folks into a caring rather than punitive custody. Non-violent offenders can often receive the treatment they need on an out-patient basis. Violent offenders can be treated on an in-patient basis. Procedures for caring for victims would also be provided.

A great load can be taken off the system by decriminalizing victimless crimes. Drug use or possession, prostitution, vagrancy, and other acts that cause no harm to another can be either left alone, or regulated and taxed, like the sale of alcohol. The laws criminalizing this kind of behavior are exceedingly Puritanical, and help no one while hurting many. Today's incarceration and punishment for such acts is pure sadism, and more shameful than the acts themselves.

Since one aim of these progressive reforms is to remove the remnants of medieval cruelty and superstition, the "combat spectacle" of the adversary system would not be needed. When the aim of a system is to help rather than to hurt, a completely different set of procedures is required. The police would do their job of investigation and arrest, as usual. But there need be no trial, nor judge, nor District Attorney, nor Public Defender.

The Police Spokesperson would provide the Chief Fact Finder, formerly known as "the judge," with the reasons for the arrest of a person. The Chief Fact Finder would then oversee an independent investigation into the facts of the case. While juries would no longer be needed, the process would be fully open to public scrutiny and participation. The inquiry would be for the scientific purpose of knowing the facts, and not for attributing any element of blame. "Guilt" and "innocence" are terms that derive their meaning from the context of "punishment;" hence, they would no longer have any use. Allegations would be either substantiated, or not substantiated. Also, because punishment is not an element of this new process, facts need not be proven, as now, "beyond a reasonable doubt." The standard currently used in civil practice, proof "by a preponderance of the evidence," would be sufficient.

Arrest procedures would be examined as part of the process. If the constable erred, the accused would go free. The Chief Fact Finder would have no sentencing power. If the accused did what he was charged with doing, then the matter would be turned over to the Diagnostic and Treatment Department (the "D.T.D.").

Persons found to have committed a serious theft, or who caused significant property damage, or engaged in some violent act would undergo a thorough personality assessment by the D.T.D. The specialists here would determine first whether in-patient or out-patient treatment would be appropriate. Then the course of treatment would be laid out. This treatment would be based solely on the unique needs of the individual offender. Menninger cites several cases in which treatment has been quite successful. Such famous cases as "the bird man of Alcatraz," and the experience of Karla Faye Tucker show that even folks who have done some terrible things can become fully human with proper guidance. Indeed, the aim of treatment would be to cultivate such a strong feeling of connection to one's brothers and sisters in the human family that further anti-social activity would become unthinkable.

Thus, in the Public Safety System the length and type of

treatment would not necessarily be related to the category of the offense. Once a person has been remanded to the D.T.D., only his or her particular needs will determine what is to be done. Only primitive thinkers believe that punishment can be made to "fit" the crime. But science knows that rehabilitation can be made to fit the individual. Thus, while a serious theft may cause a person to be brought into the system, a diagnosis may reveal such extreme hostility that in-patient treatment would be the only option for the time being. Because the safety of society comes first, no serious offender would be released from custody without the consent of the care providers, no matter what the initial offense was.

Minor offenses can be dealt with differently. A rebellious window breaker, a careless driver who coasts through a stop sign or speeds, a pizza thief, someone who spits on the sidewalk, or who lets his dog bark all day, and those who commit such other infractions of the law can be most efficiently reminded of their errors by pre-set fines, brief periods of community service, or, where appropriate, making restitution. We agree with Menninger that as a practical matter, such administrative penalties can be distinguished from sadistic punishment. Of course, the right to appeal any decision or act made in the Public Safety System would be just as available as it is today.

Our outline of the Public Safety System is an example of an ideological enhancement. The aim of the plan is to enhance the quality of life for all Americans. Because offenders would be rehabilitated prior to release, the public would feel safer. The offenders would be happier and more socially competent persons upon release;

therefore, they would be far more likely to contribute to society than to ever again offend against it.

This Public Safety System would function as an instrumental enhancement in the lives of individuals. That is, persons would be processed through the system, not for the thrill of spectators, but for the enrichment of their own lives. The role of the police would be transformed from the image of the "tough cop," to something like the far more civil "London bobby." From street to courthouse to treatment center, suspects and offenders would not be valued instrumentally, as grist for the punishment mill. Instead, people would be treated with the respect they deserve; in other words; all persons would always be treated with positive regard.

Humanity defines the concept of "justice" for itself. The continuation of the medieval meaning of "justice," as public punishment for doing a forbidden act, is also the continuation of an uncured medieval social sickness. Science and logic can help us to heal ourselves. A value healthy people would redefine "justice." Indeed, underlying the Public Safety System is a new concept of "justice" as "compassion-plus."

In the Public Safety System, "justice" entails compassion, plus the use of governmental power so as to benefit everyone in society. Police power used to take offenders into protective custody benefits all. Power used to hold and/or monitor a person who is under treatment for his or her anti-social acts until he or she is healed, benefits all.

"Justice" includes answering the cry for help from a wounded brother or sister. This kind of "justice" understands that he or she has been unable to understand and control the impulse to lash out in anti-social conduct, and that such acts are an expression of his or her inner confusion and pain. "Justice" entails using the vast resources of our highly advanced society to help our brothers and sisters to heal. Healed people do not repeat their anti-social errors. Scientific knowledge empowers our society to re-socialize those whose original socialization has failed.

Re-socialized individuals will have a new self-awareness, and a new knowledge of how to spot within themselves, and manage, their potentially anti-social impulses. For some this may mean adhering to their prescribed medication regime, to be monitored by their caregivers. Others may only need to meet regularly with a specialized support group.

Progressives, and surely all other Americans, believe in the First Amendment's protection of religious freedom. But our faith in the constitutional separation of church and state also requires us to treat anti-social behavior, not with the religious conceptions of "evil" and "punishment," but as a public health problem amenable to management with the tools of science. Because poverty is a major producer of individual suffering and of crime, poverty is also a public health problem. With the articulation of progressive logic, we can now see that correcting contradictions of value logic is the key to healing social ills. Thus, our society needs progressives to formulate a program for healing poverty, one of our country's main social maladies. Doing that, along with decriminalizing victimless crimes, would take a great load off the Public Safety System, and enable the system to work in depth on the few who will need its services.

Conclusion:
Getting It On

FDR and Jesus

If our country has ever produced "a man for all seasons," it is Franklin Delano Roosevelt. Historians debate endlessly over the so-called "great man theory." Howard Zinn has made a career of rebelling against the notion that one person can be singled out as the leader of an epoch. But his efforts fail at the feet of FDR.

Without Roosevelt's leadership, there would have been no New Deal. All the ideas in the New Deal were around before FDR first ran for the presidency in 1928. But the scattered proponents of these ideas were impotent in their isolation. Roosevelt pulled it all together and almost magically turned mere ideas into real legislation. His actions were manifestations of progressive logic. He used his personal command of political power to attack the points at which government was expressing the most negative regard for the people. He reversed the indifference to suffering that the Social Darwinists had instituted under Hoover. He led Congress to express positive regard for the people with a gleaming cascade of helpful laws.

When mothers with dependent children had no one to provide for them during the Great Depression, he gave them AFDC. When children's lives were being ruined by long hours of tedious toil in unprogressive states, he gave them The Fair Labor Standards Act. That law also gave working mothers more time off and a higher wage.

When young men filled the streets and went idle because they could not find jobs, he gave them work building roads, bridges, schools, and rural and urban water systems. He had them planting trees, taking industrial training, and even paid them for art projects such as painting murals and photographing the countryside.

When those who worked suddenly lost their jobs through no fault of their own and could no longer support their families, he gave them unemployment insurance. He also gave the nation the Social Security Act as insurance against poverty in old age. When workers could not form unions because the Robber Barons of industry crushed their every effort, he gave the workers The National Labor Relations Board to include unions at the bargaining table. He also had the use of injunctions to stop strikes outlawed — even though he had been born to the upper class!

To stop greedy bankers from foreclosing on home mortgages, he created housing agencies to lend homeowners money and to guarantee their home loans. To save people from having to live in slums, he had the U.S. Housing Authority created to assist local governments to build new public housing.

At that time, most Americans lived on farms. Under Hoover, the greedy bankers were foreclosing on these, too. FDR also had agencies set up to come to the aid of farmers. They were given low cost federal loans so they could keep on farming, or buy their own farm if they were mere sharecroppers.

This was progressive logic in action, and that list is not even half of it!

To their discredit, the Supreme Court Justices donned their henchman hats and ran behind Roosevelt knocking down nearly every major law he had passed. But FDR was undaunted. He had Congress pass all the laws again! Then he showed even more spunk. He stood up to those black robed henchmen of the superrich and threatened to pack the Court with his own people if the Old Justices kept it up. The cowards backed down, and the New Deal continued.

Who has done more for America than FDR? Certainly not Jesus Christ of Nazareth. All he has done for us is to supply both sides of the Civil War with a supportive ideology, like an unscrupulous arms dealer. He was no help to FDR. Indeed, Father Caughlin used Christian ideology to oppose the New Deal as the product of communism and the anti-Christ. All the progress that was made during the New Deal resulted from the people backing Roosevelt and acting together for the common good of the country. There was no "divine intervention," nor any need for it. FDR proved what Lincoln said; "with the support of the people, we can do anything."

Indeed, the use of religious rhetoric is unhelpful to progressive politics. One reason is that it does no good. People in both North and South prayed all day, every day for an end to the war. But only Sherman's March to the Sea made it happen. Prayers are rubber crutches.

Far worse, is that any Christian rhetoric used in politics opens the door to the fanatical right. Those liberal preachers who use religious language in public discourse are Judas Goats. By legitimizing the use of such rhetoric in political dialogue, they are providing more aid to the advocates of "Christianocracy" than to us progressives.

If Christian liberals want to be helpful to progressive politics, they should voluntarily refrain from the use of religious rhetoric to either praise or criticize public policy. This would show their commitment to the separation of church and state which is one of the founding principles of our nation. It would also isolate the Christian extremists who want the Bible to be the basis of American law and policy. Stigmatized by their own language, they would lose public support. Our government was originally, and wisely, intended to entail a secular policy-making process. Madison's notes on the Constitutional Convention in Philadelphia show that none of the Founders sought to make the Bible the basis of the Constitution. All their arguments were secular. Our country, indeed the world, would be better served if the people of all faiths saved their religious rhetoric for church, temple, mosque, or synagogue, and kept it out of the public square. Religion and politics can only be a deadly brew.

The Elections Subsystem

If all persons always deserve positive regard, then all the systems that comprise a society should always serve the people whom such systems impact. People should never be reduced to the instrumental value of resources used only to support a particular system. This principle of value applies across the board, including the criminal justice system, the systems of slavery and child labor, and other systems within the economy as well as to the health care system, the elections system, and so on.

A society is a complex set of systems, or subsystems. The elements of each system can be observed and described. Its origins and the social consequences of its operation can be known by the same method. Once the factual processes are known, they can be interpreted for the values they manifest. As we saw in the previous section, the values a social system manifests are generally the values intended by those who maintain the system. Once these values have been determined, they can be measured against the principles of progressive logic. Where contradictions are found, alternative means for correcting them can be proposed and discussed.

What, if any, action is to be taken is a political decision, ideally to be made through the democratic process. Politics is the art of the possible. Social systems are often held in place by a balance of opposed and conjoined pressures. Changing these configurations is a practical matter that depends upon numerous variables. The struggles between interests are what ultimately determine what can and should be done.

Our purpose for this essay is not to present a complete inventory of all the value contradictions in the many subsystems of American society. We seek here only to articulate the principles of progressive logic, with a few illustrations of its application. A complete analysis of the value contradictions in today's health care system, for example, would require an essay just on that subject. Suffice it to say briefly that such an analysis would show a system that bills itself as "the best health care system in the world." To any one who is familiar with the system's actual operation, however, that sounds like a claim made by P. T. Barnum (the 19th Century huckster who called his circus "the greatest show on earth"). In practice, our health care system is one of the best profit making businesses "on earth." HMOs and pharmaceutical companies are among the wealthiest corporations in the world.

That system uses the people as resources for corporate profit making. Persons without money or medical insurance are not served by the system, but are disregarded by it. Under progressive logic, all Americans deserve a health care system just as good as the one now enjoyed by our elected officials in Congress. They choose their doctor, and receive all the medical attention and medication they need, for free! The current health care practices manifest Congress's true apportionment of positive regard. The already obscenely rich corporations are Congress's top priority. Congress allows the system to exploit the people for profit, and Congress does nothing to help those without money or insurance who are barred from entry into the "the best health care system in the world."

What accounts for Congress's distorted sense of value? One reason explains it all. Most of our elected officials are helplessly and hopelessly dependent upon private contributions to fund their campaigns for public office. While there are several millionaires in Congress, especially in the Senate, very few pay their campaign costs out of their own pockets. Anyway, to their credit, voters resent rich guys trying to buy their way into office. Most of these efforts fail (e.g., Ross Perot, Steve Forbes, Michael Huffington, et al). Washington is so awash in money that the rich do not need to rely on their own funds. Instead, nearly all of our elected officials depend almost entirely upon private contributions to fund their campaigns for public office. Of course, the HMOs and pharmaceuticals are among the biggest givers. That is why Congress dashed Bill and Hillary's efforts to have their health care reform measure passed in the 1990's. Through our Congress, the corporations can overrule the president!

Only a Congress that has no need of private money can be depended upon to serve the public interest. Hence, all armchair and lounge proclamations about what reforms are needed will come to naught unless and until our current money-driven election system is dismantled and replaced by a fully public funded process. Tinkering won't do. We need a new system.

The history of progressive efforts to tinker with the election system is a sad tale of repeated failures. Consider first the presidential election system. Holding primaries in the states was a progressive device meant to empower the people to screen presidential candidates. While taking some power away from the old time party "bosses," that "reform" only further empowered the superrich. Competing in primaries costs millions.

Now, candidates are no longer chosen in smoke filled hotel rooms during conventions. Instead, the conventions have become rubber stamps for a prior and covert process, a pre-primary process. That is, two or more years before the primaries get underway the hopefuls begin begging for contributions from the superrich. No hopeful, not even a millionaire, has a chance of success in the primaries without ten to twenty million dollars in hand, to fund his primary campaigns. Even the candidates with that much money must also have the ability to raise more than $125,000,000 for the presidential election campaign. Usually, the guy who raises the most pre-primary money turns out to be the winner of the November election two or three years later. The November vote is a charade, coming long after the real decision-making.

Congressional elections are a miniature replica of the presidential election process. Without ten million dollars, the average senator will not be able to pay for an election or reelection campaign. In big and competitive states, the costs are far higher. Campaigns for House seats can cost five million dollars or more, every two years! No wonder the 535 members of Congress put most of their working day not into the public's business, but into fund raising.

Clearly, our election process is rigged to produce a government that gives its positive regard not to the people but to the superrich. A privileged cadre of 250,000 or so big contributors constitutes the "Master Race" for America. The two-party system is a façade, creating the illusion of choice for the voter. The facts are that the candidates for each party have usually been selected long before Election Day by the wealthy few. This is the result of a one hundred year long history of failed efforts to reform the federal election system. After every reform effort, campaign costs and spending have gone up, and the grip of the superrich on the system has tightened.

Congress's most recent "reform" promises to continue that trend. The cynically named "Help America Vote Act of 2002" is putting up billions of taxpayer dollars to reimburse the states for buying thousands of new electronic voting machines from private companies. These are the machines that made the 2004 Ohio vote for Bush look like a fix. The companies manufacturing these machines are often active in politics, hire lobbyists, and sometimes are highly partisan.

Those who have voted on these machines know the problems. Such equipment is programmed to show on the screen that your vote was recorded as cast. But the machines can also have a secret program in them to actually record your vote according to the programmer's desire. Rather than the happy feeling of having participated in the democratic process, you may leave the polling place with a sickening uncertainty as to how your vote was really counted, if counted at all! That was one of the problems in Ohio, and in other voting districts in states where these machines were used. (County election officials can check the codes in these machines, but their programming sophistication is less than that of the pros, and they lack the staff to check all the machines. Also, some machines may be open to re-programming after inspection by remote control.)

Under the guise of "helping America to vote," Congress may be leading the country towards a crisis in election legitimacy. While a voter may never know if a machine is rigged to favor Republicans or Democrats, he or she can be sure that if the machine has been "adjusted," it will not be to favor any third party or any candidate who truly represents the people. In most cases, only the servants of the superrich will win.

We progressives would do well to plan a voting system which, when used by voters, will leave them feeling the joys of participating in the democratic process. Such joy cannot be felt when a voter knows that the candidates have been pre-selected by the ruling few, and when the voter leaves the voting booth wondering how, or if, his or her vote has been counted. To be fully democratic, an election would have to be open to all candidates and parties without favoritism. Secondly, these candidates would have to be free of dependency upon private funding. Public funding is needed so that even the poorest of candidates has an equal opportunity to have his or her voice heard in the campaign process. Surely, in the Age of the Internet this can be done.

Even if modern technology is able to produce such a truly democratic system, there is one old fashion obstacle to get around. It's the Supreme Court. Once again the Court has been caught with its hands around its ankles. In *Buckley v. Valeo*, the High Court sought to please not one or other of the two major parties, but the contributing class that controls them both. This opinion declares, in effect, that "money is speech," and under the First Amendment government cannot limit the freedom of speech. Therefore, money spent in support of candidates, parties, or causes by wealthy individuals and private groups, such as "political action committees," or PACs, cannot be limited.

These expenditures are not supposed to be coordinated with candidates or parties, but Washington lawyers know how to get around that requirement. The McCain-Feingold Act was passed to try to close some of the loopholes in the campaign finance laws. Almost instantly, groups called "527s," after a section in the tax code, popped up and began spending more money than was spent before the McCain-Feingold "reform."

Obviously, money is not speech. Money is a megaphone that empowers the superrich to dominate public discourse. The "Master Race" controls the public agenda. They impose their materialistic priorities upon the nation. They deliberately distract public attention from the need for laws that would enrich the quality of life of the American people. Thanks to the efforts of all three branches of our government, the candidates of the superrich win almost every time.

With most of the elected officials in the U.S. government against us, we progressives have our work cut out for us. The only way we will be able to truly democratize our election process is to enact a constitutional amendment.[20] Such an amendment will also be needed to institute the Public Safety System. Without these amendments, the Supreme Court will have the power to subvert our progress, and it will surely use that power. Once our reforms become a part

---

[20] A detailed presidential election reform proposal can been seen at *www.empathicscience.org* .

of the Constitution, that Court cannot rule our amendments "unconstitutional."

To have the needed constitutional amendments proposed for a vote will require a progressive "super majority" of 67% in the House and Senate. But even that will not be sufficient. We must also elect progressive majorities in "three fourths of the several States," under Article Five of the U.S. Constitution. That is the number of states required to ratify our amendments. This is a very tall order, but it can be done.

Our Best Method of Attack

By articulating the principles of progressive logic we have made the unconscious conscious; that is, we have made explicit the intuitive sense of value that has moved American progressives for at least the past two hundred years. The reader may check our claim, to have brought the implicit into consciousness, against his or her own value intuition. Our statement of progressive logic should "ring true" for every person of humane sensibilities.

However, we must realistically accept the fact that numerous people live with value disabilities, or value blindness. Those American voters who feel a bit fuzzy about their values need at least the appearance of intellectual clarity to give them some relief from their confusion. Many of these people vote in the conservative block solely because the Christian extremists seem so sure of their values, and progressive candidates and activists seem so divided and bewildered as to their values. The 2004 presidential election illustrates the point. John Kerry's apparent value malleability (a hunter on TV one day, a humanitarian the next, for the war one day, against it the next), made him look uncertain about what he believes in, and opportunistic. George Bush II's apparent value certainty (cut taxes for the rich, and an unflagging support for the war) gave him the image of being a value leader (despite his use of deception to garner support for the war in Iraq). In a presidential election contest between value decisiveness and value indecision, decisiveness will generally win. Having a leader with some semblance of value certainty is a powerful emotional need for many people.

Now that progressive logic has been articulated, it can be taught. Progressive logic will provide the American voter with several benefits that our conservative opponents cannot match. One, as we have said, is a far higher degree of clarity in value thinking. Our logic is clear, easy to understand, and hard to refute. Once our basic premise is accepted, any rational mind can critically examine the policy conclusions that progressives draw from that premise. Also, progressive criticisms of existing policies, laws, and programs can be checked for logical consistency by anyone. Progressive logic encourages independent thinking, not sheepish following.

Another benefit of progressive logic is its human sensitivity. Progressive logic is always humane. Republican Party rhetoric and policies are rarely humane. Their "free market" philosophy, for example, assumes the validity of Social Darwinism; i.e., that "the survival of the fittest" is a "law of nature." But as Harvard historian, Gabriel Kolko makes clear, there are no "free markets." Our economy consists of markets dominated by self-serving elites who regard themselves as "the fittest." Herbert Hoover illustrated the inhumanity of this view by his refusal to use federal power and resources to help the American people during the Great Depression.

FDR was elected president four times by the American voters precisely because of his compassion and willingness to use the government to help the people. No other person in our history has been elected president more than twice. FDR embodies the ideal of progressive justice. That the majority of voters elected FDR president four times shows the depth of humanitarian feeling of the American voters.

Progressive logic can provide the American people with the conceptual tools they need to stay consistent with their humanitarian predisposition. Their current support of the Republicans at the polls is due more to the failure of the Democrats to provide value leadership than it is to a failure of human feeling in the voters. American identity with the Christian religion is, like Mark Twain said of the Mississippi River, a mile wide, but only an inch deep. For most, that identity is an insurance policy. They identify themselves as "Christians" just in case that scary, vengeful bearded guy in the sky really exists. The Republicans have exploited this fear by associating their candidates and policies with the Christian religion. In the absence of any intelligible alternative, voting

Christian Republican seems to be the safest thing to do for one's soul in the afterlife!

However, an earthly humanitarian feeling runs much deeper among Americans than does their identity with Christianity. Progressive activists and candidates need only educate the people about progressive logic to drive a huge wedge into the conservative voting block. There are several reasons for this. Simply telling people about progressive logic necessitates addressing them as rational beings. Political discourse in America is generally conducted in a manner that insults the intelligence of most Americans. Small wonder that most people who are eligible to vote don't bother. Sound bites, slogans, and TV ads, meant to by-pass reason and to manipulate emotion, draw a well-deserved contempt for "politics" among Americans. Many rightly resent this abuse of the democratic process.

Addressing people as rational beings who can learn new ideas and who can think for themselves would show the people a degree of respect, indeed honor, for their intellects that rarely occurs in political discourse. In addition to the solid content of progressive logic, this manner of delivery would of itself bring in support for progressive candidates and causes. Michael Lerner's studies of working class people have shown that the self-righteous blaming rhetoric of Democratic Party elites in the past has tended to drive many white working people over to the Republicans. Many of them feel unjustly criticized for the inequities suffered by women and minorities in the past. Progressive logic provides an opportunity for the left to change its rhetorical style from moralizing to value reasoning.

The smugness and superiority of moralizers offends the democratic sensitivities of many Americans. But value reasoning would acknowledge those sensitivities. Logical discourse requires an equality of participants. That Great Gadfly, Socrates of Athens always used logic in his discussions, and never resorted to moral superiority to win by intimidation. Why not follow his example? Such value reasoning would not appeal to Christian conceptions of "good and evil," as dictated by their All Mighty God. Instead, it would appeal to the uniquely American conscience that has been cultivated in our culture over the past two centuries.

Contained within the American self-image is a sense of decency. It is not a sentimental gushiness, nor the guilt of the rich, but a pioneer's willingness to help those who will help themselves, and a desire for fair play and equal opportunity. The American conscience, not Christian dogma, prevailed in the drive for abolition. Even after a terrible, bitter, heart wrenching civil war, American decency led General Grant to allow Lee and his soldiers to keep their swords, small arms, and horses when the South surrendered at Appomattox. Grant knew the men would need these items back on the farm, or for settling in the West.

The richest metaphor for the sense of American decency is that of "GI Joe" from WWI and WWII. We went "over there" twice to help the Europeans fight to preserve their freedom. Towards the end of WWII, as the Russians were closing in on Berlin, German soldiers raced to surrender to the Americans. They knew who would treat them more decently as prisoners of war.

(Needless to say, this decency is being eroded under the administration of "born again" Bush II.)

Progressive logic provides the intellectual guidance that Americans need to live true to their humanitarian conscience. We need only inform them about our logic, and many will join us. But besides providing such information, progressives can also attack the conservative block by hitting those voters in their self-images. To start voters re-thinking their behavior, progressives need only point out the value contradictions between votes for conservative candidates and policies, and the humanitarian values of the American conscience. Christian sadism is un-American!

Thomas Jefferson envisioned political participation as one element in the "pursuit of happiness." We have seen the kinds of joy that conservatives reap from their political participation. But there are other kinds of happy feelings to be had. Jefferson, and the other Founders, experienced the pleasures first hand of camaraderie among activists, and the thrill of taking bold action with the support of ones brothers and sisters, all acting together in the service of human progress.

Democracy offers everyone, not just elites, the opportunity to pursue happiness through political action. TV commercials promise happiness to those who purchase their products. Millions fall for this trick, and are ultimately disappointed. Sooner, rather than later, consumer forms of happiness end in emptiness and alienation. Democratic participation, however, can provide one with a deeper, more enduring joy. The giving of one's self can pay richer dividends than any pecuniary taking for one's self. Contributing to the creation of institutions that serve people can instill a pride in one's mind that will last for a lifetime. The struggle to make government manifest more positive regard for the people is an exact analog to the activities of our Founding Fathers during the American Revolution. Progressive action taken now can be a means by which to know the same joys in participation and the pride of accomplishment that our Founders felt.

Prodding and moving the American conscience has been the key to success for every progressive program that was ever turned into law and policy. Past experience shows that when the American people learn to see the contradictions between their values and their behavior, the behavior changes. Just consider the astonishing changes in the South as an illustration of that fact. Progressive logic now provides our side with a new opportunity to again follow that time-tested formula for success. One person can triple his or her voting power by convincing just two others to vote progressive. (Instead of one progressive vote, there will be three!) We need only master our logic, carefully craft our rhetoric to present our logic, and go out and talk to the people. Then their current voting patterns will change, and a new "Progressive Era" will begin.

Friends! Let us plan, act, and enjoy!

Bibliography

A People's History of the United States.
Howard Zinn. Harper, NY 1995.

Affluenza: The All Consuming Epidemic.
John De Graaf, et al. Berrett-Koehler, NY 2002.

The American Political Tradition.
Richard Hofstadter. Vintage, NY 1948.

Beyond Good and Evil. Friedrich Nietzsche.
Walter Kaufman, trans. Vintage, NY 1966.

The Birth of Tragedy and The Genealogy of Morals.
Friedrich Nietzsche. Francis Golffing, trans.
Doubleday, NY 1956.

The Crime of Punishment. Karl Menninger.
Viking, NY 1971.

Don't Think of an Elephant. George Lakoff.
Chelsea Green Pub. 2004.

Great Dialogues of Plato. W.H.D. Rouse, trans.
Mentor, NY 1956.

The Greening of America. Charles A. Reich.
Bantam, NY 1972.

I and Thou. Martin Buber.
Free Press, NY 1971.

Man's Search for Himself. Rollo May.
Delta, NY 1973.

Marx's Concept of Man. Erich Fromm.
Frederick Ungar, NY 1969.

The Origins of American Politics. Bernard Bailyn.
Vintage, NY 1968.

The Rise of Scientific Philosophy.
Hans Reichenbach. UC Press, Berkeley, CA 1951.

The Rhetoric of Aristotle. Lane Cooper, trans.
Appleton, NY 1960.

The Sane Society. Erich Fromm.
Fawcet, NY 1955.

The Structure of Value. Robert S. Hartman.
Southern Illinois University Press, Carbondale, Ill.
1967.

The Thought of Karl Marx. David McLellan, ed.
and trans. Harper&Row, NY 1971.

The Tyranny of Words. Stuart Chase.
Harvest Books, NY 1959.

Unpopular Essays. Bertrand Russell.
Simon and Schuster, NY 1969.

The Wealth Primary. James B. Raskin and
John Bonifaz. Center For Responsive Politics,
Washington, D.C. 1994.

APPENDIX

The formula on the cover ($S^E=I$) is taken from the formal axiology of Robert S. Hartman. In *The Structure of Value*, Hartman shows that there are three realms of value. These are the systemic, the extrinsic, and the intrinsic. The first is the realm of ideas, systems, and the conceptual. The second is the realm of things and action. The third is the realm of feeling and personal experience. Hartman provides a formal logic, for what we call "the natural order of values."

Following Henry T. Gardner, we offer one expression of that formula as: "a carefully constructed plan, well executed, can result in deep satisfaction." Gardner has also taught us the action theory that we use in the essay. That is, that people tend to act in accord with a plan for, or expectation of, some sentient benefit. Hence, the epigram "plan, act, and enjoy."

A surprising find is the existence of a sophisticated social psychology, fully expressing the natural order of values, implicit in the religious rhetoric of Helen Schucman's epic *A Course In Miracles*. This social psychology can be translated into empirical language, and then criticized and validated by the relevant scientific community.

INDEX

Note